What Others Have Said About *Together We Can!*

William Cameron Townsend, my late husband, founded Wycliffe Bible Translators. If he were alive today, he would heartily endorse *Together We Can!* The stories display his philosophy: working together with others—and his attitude and life motto: serving others in love. As you read this book, you'll be encouraged and challenged to work with and serve others.

—**Elaine Townsend**

God tells His people throughout history to remember what He has done—to worship Him for His mighty acts and be encouraged to take the next steps of faith. *Together We Can!* records the kind of stories we must remember.

They remind us that:

- We work best when we work together—our diversity, working in harmony, glorifies God, whose unity and wholeness we reflect.

- The power of God's Word to transform the life of an individual, as well as the life of a community, knows no political, economic or cultural boundaries.

- When God calls us to be His hands, feet and voice to people in every corner of the earth, He faithfully supplies all we need to enable us to obey Him.

Gather together and read these stories, and remember all that God is doing through His Word translated into the heart languages of millions. Then pray for the millions who still wait to hear the Voice of hope, redemption and life eternal speak in the language they understand best.

—**Bob Creson,**
President, Wycliffe USA

Together We Can! is a wonderful evidence of Kingdom mentality. We who are serving in mission realize we can't do the job alone. Rather, serving together is where it's at these days.

—**Fred Ely,**
SIM Deputy Director

Together We Can! brings us stories about the certainty of the truth of God's Word, changed lives, miracles, conviction of sin, and increased faith. The one thing each story has in common is the power of the Word of God. Whether it's through the process of translating it, listening to it, seeing it portrayed, or living out its truths, the Spirit makes the Word a transforming power in lives when people hear it in their own heart language. Today we see these life-transformations in greater numbers as mission organizations cooperate with one another and with the local church at home and overseas. It's called partnership, or strengthening alliances, as the stories in *Together We Can!* aptly illustrate.

—**Dr. John R. Watters,**
Executive Director, Wycliffe International

As you read *Together We Can!* you will travel around the world and view a fascinating kaleidoscope of how God powerfully works in lives of people.

—**Scott Zibell, Ph.D.,**
Geographer and Field Research Consultant for JAARS

My wife, Doris, and I have been a part of the Lovings' ministry for many years. And we count it a privilege to continue sharing in their ministry by heartily endorsing Aretta's book *Together We Can!* The stories will challenge readers to give, go and pray for missions—thereby helping fulfill Vision 2025!

—**Mel Amrine, Associate Pastor and Counselor,**
New Life Church, Little Rock, AR

The Seed Company (TSC) networks with nationals, organizations and churches in the USA and overseas, resulting in an increased number of Bible translation projects begun each year. I highly recommend my coworker Aretta Loving's book, which vividly illustrates through real life stories the effectiveness of networking!

—**Roger Garland,**
Communications Specialist, TSC

"Write what you know best," we're told. So, since I'm a lawyer, I write novels about law and lawyers. My desire is that my books will draw the reader to see Christ as the center of all life. The reader will find an element of mystery in each of my novels. In *Together We Can!* you will also find mystery—the marvelous mystery of how God's Word impacts lives!

—**Robert Whitlow, who has been called**
"the John Grisham of Christian publishing"

Do you enjoy stories? Dramatic, life changing stories? Then this book is for you. Be transported around the world and into many fascinating lives as you read about the impact of God's Word through a diversity of media.

—**Clyde Cook, President of Biola University**

Aretta's stories will take you around the world and cause you to praise God for the power in His Word to change lives!

—**Marlene Bagnull, Director of Greater Philadelphia and**
Colorado Christian Writers Conferences

Aretta_Loving @ sil.org

Yes! By God's grace —

Together
We Can!

Aretta Loving

Together We Can!
A Mosaic of Stories and Devotions Displaying the Impact of God's Word • Volume 1
by Aretta Loving

Copyright © 2007 by Aretta Loving
Dove illustrations by Louise Bass

Published by:
Harvest Day Books
an imprint of **Book Marketing Solutions, LLC**
10300 E. Leelanau Court
Traverse City, MI 49684
orders@BookMarketingSolutions.com
www.BookMarketingSolutions.com

Harvest
Day
Books

Printed in the United States of America

Loving, Aretta.
    Together we can! : a mosaic of stories and devotions displaying the
    impact of God's word / Aretta Loving ; foreword by John Perkins. --
    Traverse City, Mich. : Harvest Day Books, 2007.
        v. ; cm.
        ISBN-13: 978-0-9790834-4-0
        ISBN-10: 0-9790834-4-3
    Stories collected from the mission field around the world.
    Scriptures and devotions relate to the stories. Each chapter
    concludes with a brief prayer, meditation, and reflection.
        Includes bibliographical references.
        1. Missionary stories. 2. Missionaries. 3. Christian life.
    4. Meditations. I. Perkins, John. II. Title.
BV2087 .L68 2007
266-dc22   0703

This book is available at:
www.ReadingUp.com

Together We Can!

A Mosaic *of* Stories and Devotions
Displaying the Impact *of* God's Word

Aretta Loving

Foreword by Dr. John Perkins

——————— VOLUME ONE ———————

Harvest
Day
Books

Traverse City • Michigan

Dedication

I dedicate this book to all who graciously gave me permission to publish their stories, and to the organizations they represent. The time they gave to check the accuracy of my numerous revisions, and the updating and verifying of details has helped ensure an accurate recounting of their experiences.

Contents

Acknowledgements

Two persons exercised their gift of using "the red pen"—or the computer's red track changes—on my manuscript. To them I say, first of all, "Ouch!" But I quickly add, "Thank you!" to Ed Loving, my husband, and to my coworker Carol Brinneman. Both gave much thought and valuable time from their busy schedules to make these stories more readable.

A big "Thank you!" goes to my publisher. Tom White not only is publishing *Together We Can!* but since he has a heart for missions, he is also excited about publishing it.

And a "Thank you!" to Ilene Stankiewicz, Harvest Day Books editor, for her valuable editing of the manuscript, which has made the stories in *Together We Can!* more understandable to an audience not familiar with the world of mission.

Foreword

by Dr. John M. Perkins

Aretta Loving's book is a beautiful testimony to the authentication of the Bible as the Word of God. The writer of the book of Hebrews says, "For the word of God is living and powerful, and sharper than any two-edged sword, piercing even to the division of soul and spirit, and of joints and marrow, and is a discerner of the thoughts and intents of the heart" (Hebrews 4:12, NKJV).

Almost 50 years ago, when I first heard the Word of God, that is how it affected me. Through His Word, God's Spirit showed me that I was lost, that I was a sinner. He showed me that Jesus had come to save me from my sins. That long ago morning when I heard the Word, it seemed as if God knew my deepest needs. Because I grew up without a mother and without a strong father, I grew up with a huge lack in my life. And that's where God met me; He met me at my greatest need—the need and desire to be loved.

After I came to know that I was loved by Him, my greatest desire was to love this God back. And I so much wanted to understand what He was saying to me in His Word. But with my meager amount of education, I found it very difficult to read and understand that Word. One morning feeling deeply burdened by this, out of distress and pain I prayed, "Lord, please help me understand your Word. If you will help me to understand it, I will preach it for the rest of my life."

Maybe I was somehow trying to bribe God. But God is merciful and always hears His children when we call out to Him in our pain. From then on, as I read the Bible I understood what I was reading. It seemed as though a tape recorder was in my head imprinting the words in my mind—and those words are still there! They're there when I need them, there for me to pull up and use.

Not only did God give me a desire to study His Word, He also gave me a desire to be faithful in teaching His Word to "faithful men who will be able to teach others also" (2 Timothy 2:2, NKJV). For more than 50 years now, I have worked on teaching and motivating other people to carry the good news of the Gospel around the world.

I know that God is pleased when He sees us doing that. When He sees us working together to carry that Gospel around the world, when churches and Christian organizations work together, we please God. And we show mission at its best. We show God's great heart of love to the world, because mission is on the heart of God; He sent His Son to earth.

Mission is on the heart of our Lord Jesus; He obeyed and came down to reach people like you and me who were lost and lacking love. And just before he returned to His Father, He told His followers to go and make disciples of all nations (Matthew 28:19, NKJV).

Mission is on the heart of the Holy Spirit; He changes our desires and even our minds so we can understand God's Word and then become "witnesses . . . in Jerusalem, and in all Judea and Samaria, and to the end of the earth" (Acts 1:8, NKJV).

Mission should be on the heart of every Christian. And if that Christian is seeking to please God, it is.

Mission is at the heart of the Bible, which is God's Word. Jesus said, "Go into all the world and preach the gospel to every creature" (Mark 16:15, NKJV). In *Together We Can!* you'll meet people—even groups of people—whose lives have been changed or somehow impacted by that good news we're told to go and preach. You'll meet:

- Peng, a young man in Laos, whose father was a shaman. Peng was supposed to follow in his father's footsteps. But when working in his fields, he had done some hard thinking. *Somewhere a Good Spirit must exist. Sunshine and rain make our rice grow. And the world is so beautiful. Did this all just happen? Or is there someone who caused it to happen?* Peng heard a rumor: "The white people in town claim they know something about a Good Spirit who can deliver from the power of evil spirits." *Is this really true?* he wondered. His wondering led him to the home of missionaries ...

- Karen, a missionary kid who came to Christ when five-years old. After she grew up, she felt she didn't have a "terrific testimony" like some of the women in her Bible study had. One was an ex-drug addict. Another had divorced, and later had an abortion. And another woman had decided she would prove that the Bible was not true. But her plan to prove that it was untrue backfired. God showed Karen that He had saved her *from*, rather than *out of*, the things those women had gone through. Karen realized that her story was "no less exciting, no less a testimony of God's grace" than the stories of the women in her Bible study.

- A team of men and women in Australia, first introduced by the sentence: "Wielding a newly sharpened axe, Maratja and the women take turns chopping until the tree falls apart, exposing a hollowed inside flowing with *guku* (wild honey)." After they attend a translation course, they become part of a team translating the Bible into their own language. They describe techniques learned at that course as "sharpening the axe so we can cut for the sweetest honey."

- A serial killer who threw himself down on his knees and cried out to God to forgive him. "I got up, at peace for the first time in my thirty-three years," he says. And gradually old things left his life and new things entered—just as the Bible says in 2 Corinthians 5:17. Today he serves Jesus in prison. "There's a ripe harvest of hungry hearts here, and this is my mission field," he says.

- A missionary couple who went and lived among a group of people on "scattered islands-of-jungle in an everglade of the Amazon basin," as the story says. After two years of studying the people's language and culture, the first verse from the Bible they decided to translate was John 14:6— Jesus' claim that "I am the way, the truth, and the life. No one comes to the Father except through Me" (NKJV). Those people, prepared by the Holy Spirit in a unique way, all turned to Jesus.

- An abusive man who taught himself to read after he discovered that the Gospel of Luke had been translated into his language. He stopped beating his wife, and night after night, sat reading that Gospel. "He's a changed man!" his wife declared.

- Two brothers from El Tambo, who left their high-in-the-Andes hometown, and settled in the fertile lowlands to homestead government-assigned land. After listening to a Gospel broadcast each morning for several weeks, they came to Jesus and received His forgiveness for sin. They felt God told them to go back to their own people, just as He told me to go back to my people.

You will meet others in this book—my story is among them—and all the stories tell how God's Word changes lives. And it's happened as we have worked together to preach and teach the Gospel.

[signature]

Preface

Together. From the day Jesus sent His followers out two-by-two to neighboring villages to tell about the kingdom of God, the plan has been that we not be "Lone Rangers" as we spread the good news. We need to work with others, together fulfilling our mission.
—Tricia Scribner

"Together We Can!" Wycliffe chose those three simple, yet profound, words as the theme for their 1999 triennial International Conference. Dr. John Watters, at that time Executive Director of Wycliffe Bible Translators International, presented Vision 2025 for adoption by the floor: "Because we believe people should have God's message as soon as possible, we aim to see a Bible translation program begun in all remaining languages that need one by 2025."

Dr. Watters and those at the conference realized that the fulfilling of Vision 2025—a seemingly impossible task—could not be accomplished alone. It would require working together with partners worldwide in an even greater measure than previously: other missions and churches, both at home and overseas.

Today, working together—most often called *partnership*—is a major topic in mission council meetings. At times, it's referred to as sharing or facilitating (especially regarding technology and information); forming or strengthening alliances; teamworking or networking; joining hands . . . Other times, showing that it is a "together-thing," it's called coming together, banding together, working together, strategizing together, serving together . . . SIM has even renamed its quarterly publication *Serving In Mission Together*.

Working together is not something new. John and Helen Ellenberger, Bible translators with The Christian and Missionary Alliance in the 1950s, speak of "The Missions Fellowship." They explain: "To see God's Word spread in Irian Jaya (now Papua), nine missions banded together.[1] They provided staff to other missions during annual conferences—special speakers, kitchen chefs, and Vacation Bible School teachers for the children."

So, by whatever name, mission organizations have a history of cooperation. And today a renewed zeal to work together is blossoming among those who translate the Bible, those who produce and distribute films, DVDs and cassettes, those who focus on evangelizing and church planting or education, those who print and place Scripture materials produced by other missions.

The stories in *Together We Can!* display the power of God's Word in lives around the world. Story after story testifies to the truth of a statement made by an Asian mission leader: "No Christian group can walk by itself. If we all work together, we get more done."

[1]"The Missions Fellowship" included Asia Pacific Christian Mission (now Pioneers of Australia); Australian Baptist (now Global interAction); The Christian and Missionary Alliance; Missionary Aviation Fellowship; Regions Beyond Missionary Union (now World Team); The Evangelical Alliance Mission; Unevangelized Fields Mission (now CrossWorld); and two Missions of the Dutch Reformed Churches.

Explanation of Terms

Wycliffe (WBT), SIL, and **JAARS** are associate organizations.

- The mission of Wycliffe Bible Translators in each home country is to assist the church in making disciples of all nations through Bible translation.

- SIL International facilitates language-based development and serves the peoples of the world through research, linguistic training, translation, and literacy.

- JAARS, the technical support and training subsidiary of SIL International, serves the worldwide Bible translation movement with quality technical support services and resources.

The Seed Company and **Wycliffe Associates USA**

- These two organizations are partner organizations with Wycliffe Bible Translators.

Back-translation

- In order for a consultant to check Scripture translated into a language he or she does not know, someone who knows that language does a somewhat literal (but free enough for the consultant to understand) translation of that Scripture into a language the consultant does know. That translation is called a "back-translation."

God's Word

- The terms "God's Word," "the Word of God," and "Scripture" or "Scriptures," when used in this book, always refer to the Bible—either the Old Testament, the New Testament, a Gospel, an Epistle, or even as small a portion as one verse from the Bible.

Both the author and the publisher of this book subscribe to the view that the Bible is the inspired words of God. They were recorded as described in 2 Peter 1:20-21: "Above all, you must understand that no prophecy of Scripture came about by the prophet's own interpretation. For prophecy never had its own origin in the will of man, but men spoke from God as they were carried along by the Holy Spirit."

Prologue

The Singing Wells of Borana

Partnership is the ability to work together toward a common vision; the ability to direct individual accomplishments toward organized objectives. It is the fuel that allows common people to attain uncommon results . . . Simply put, it is less "me" and more "we".
-Anonymous

Using simple tools, Borana men living in the Marsabit district of Kenya, East Africa, dig wells by hand that are 20 or 30 feet deep—sometimes deeper—in rocky, dry river beds. Once the well is dug, a team of men stand on wooden ladders inside the well. From man to man, they pass up leather *okhales* filled with water. And at that most gratifying moment—as the precious life-giving liquid is passed upward—the men sing, building up a dynamic rhythm that lightens the hard work. They sing in praise of cattle, in praise of the owner of the well, and in praise of their neighbors who own the largest herds of cattle. They sing to celebrate the life-giving water in an arid desert region. Then, at the top of the well, men take the *okhales* and pour the water into a wooden trough where hundreds of cattle quench their thirst.

Similarly, for those reaching people without Christ, the Living Water, no one person can do the job alone; it's a team effort. Every believer in Christ Jesus can have the privilege of getting that life-giving Water to the thirsty; however, many hands are needed to bring the Water to the surface and make it available to the peoples of the world.

Yet in mission, how easy to only notice the people who "pour water into the trough" (the Bible translators or church planters, and those who directly support such people with their technical and professional skills). Those who "draw the water" and do the hard work of "passing up the *okhale*" (people who encourage, give and pray) are often overlooked. But as we serve together in "passing up the *okhale*" or actually "pouring water into the trough," we share the joy of seeing people drinking the life-giving Water.

Yes, together we can!

1

The Creation Story
Brings Forth New Life

As the vehicle for the living Word of God, the Bible has within itself the power for creation and redemption.

— Donald W. McCullough

Like most village people in Ghana, West African, Awalo was a virtual slave to fetish priests. Every aspect of people's lives was controlled by these men. They had knowledge on how to contact the ancestral spirits. In trouble? One of them performs a dance to persuade the spirits to take your side. Need money? "I'll gladly sell you a charm that will bring money your way," one tells you. Sick? An herbalist cooks up a magic potion to heal you.

The priests taught that spirits resided in trees, animals and rocks. If Awalo pleased these spirits, they would not harm him. In fact, they might even help him. "I constantly appeased the spirits," he says, "but I had no peace. I was always afraid I'd displease them. Sometimes my fear even caused me to become sick."

Then one day, Awalo received a Bible from Bible League.[1] Holding it in his hands, he breathed, "It's written in my language!" Eagerly, he started reading, beginning with the book of Genesis. He read about God creating the earth and everything in it. *Since God controls all life, He controls my life. And I can trust Him to care for me, heal me and guide me*, he reasoned. "I knew then that I should no longer follow the fetish priests. I should worship God the Creator."

Though Awalo had heard about Jesus, the Holy Spirit used the creation story to lead him out of the darkness and bondage of the fetish priests' demands into spiritual light. The Genesis creation account put him in touch, personally, with God, the One who created light.

One of the verses of "I Heard the Angels Sing," a song by Ellis Deibler, says:

> *They say the angels sang to praise the Lord of glory*
> *When God made light begin to glow;*
> *They saw the earth established, mountains rise from valleys,*
> *And heard the Lord tell all the plants to grow.*
> *But angels held their breath when God created people,*
> *Seeing them turn their backs on such a God of love;*
> *They wished that we would join them, praising God the Father,*
> *Singing in God's choir up above.*

That day Awalo joined the angels singing praise to the great Creator God who had led him out of darkness into the light!

PRAYER

Father, thank you for Bible League's commitment to place Bibles and New Testaments with people, then disciple them. Pray that those who receive Bibles will read God's Word and come to know the One who created all things.

MEDITATION

It is I who made the earth and created mankind upon it. My own hands stretched out the heavens; I marshaled their starry hosts. (Isaiah 45:12)

For by him all things were created: things in heaven and on earth, visible and invisible . . . all things were created by him and for him. (Colossians 1:16)

You are worthy, our Lord and God, to receive glory and honor and power, for you created all things, and by your will they were created and have their being. (Revelation 4:11)

REFLECTION

Most of us have never met someone enslaved to a fetish priest. But we have relatives, friends, or acquaintances who, like Awalo, are enslaved—enslaved to money, TV, sports, lovely clothes . . . Have I considered giving someone a Bible and asking God to use His Word to set that person free?

---

[1]Bible League provides funds for the publication of Scripture translated by Wycliffe and other organizations. They also place Scriptures with people. See Appendix B for a fuller account of Bible League's ministry.

2

Sunshine, Rain, and Spirit Strings

Natural understanding reveals that there is a God, Who is Lord and sovereign over everything, Who is therefore to be held in awe, loved, praised, called upon, trusted in, and served with all our heart, soul, and might. The acceptable way of worshipping the true God is established by God Himself. God's revealed will so defines and outlines proper worship that neither the imagination and devices of men nor the suggestions of Satan are to be followed. God is not worshipped under any visible representation or in any other way than that prescribed in Holy Scripture.
— **The Westminster Confession of Faith, Chapter 21**

"He's the One I want to follow!" the young man cried out.

Just that week, John and Dorothy Davis, OMF missionaries to Laos, had prayed, "Lord, please send us a courageous person! One who will faithfully follow you and become a light to this dark area when we leave."

Dorothy was having health problems, so they were taking a home assignment in the United States. Only a few people had professed their faith in Christ as the Davises had faithfully preached God's Word. But, sadly, those few had soon returned to their traditional ways—appeasing evil spirits.

Unknown to this discouraged couple, Peng, the young man standing before them, had done some hard thinking as he worked his fields. *Somewhere a Good Spirit must exist. Sunshine and rain make our rice grow. And the world is so beautiful. Did this all just happen? Or is there someone who caused it to happen?*

Peng's father, a shaman, had spent his life appeasing evil spirits, and Peng was slated to follow in his father's footsteps. But Peng heard a rumor: "The white people in town claim they know something about a Good Spirit who can deliver people from the power of the evil spirits."

Is this really true? he wondered. His wondering led him to the home of the Davises the very week of their very specific prayer.

John explained the Gospel carefully to Peng. "Jesus is the Son of the living God and He has broken the power of evil spirits," he said. It was then that Peng cried out, "He's the One I want to follow!"

John noted strings around Peng's wrists. "If you want to follow Jesus, you must cut off your spirit strings," John told him. "You cannot appease the spirits and follow Jesus at the same time."

"But how can I get home safely if I cut them off? The spirits might kill me on the way," Peng countered. "Let me live here with you, then I'll cut them off."

John laid his pocketknife on the chair beside Peng. "Jesus is more powerful than the spirits," John patiently explained. "He will go with you and protect you if you trust Him." Minutes ticked by. Sweat broke out on Peng's forehead. Finally, Peng reached out and picked up the knife . . .

Looking down at the crumpled strands, he called out, "Oh, Jesus, I did it! Now this man says you are greater than the evil spirits. Please chase them out of my life. Protect me and forgive my sins." Then, with a great sigh of relief, Peng threw the strings onto the floor, behind him.

A friend helped Peng learn to read, and he avidly studied the leaflets the Davises left him. Near the end of the rainy season women missionaries arrived in the town near his village. "Peng visited often and began to study God's Word with us," says Rosemary Watson.[1] Though the Bible studied was in the Laotian language, the women gave him gospel records in his own language. During the dry season Peng attended a Bible camp for teenagers. The next wet season—rice planting time—Peng's father allotted him five rice fields to plant. He was permitted to commit these to Jesus' protection instead of making a sacrifice to the evil spirits.

"Yes," Peng decided, "this One who has protected my rice fields from damage by storms and gave sunshine and rain to produce an abundant harvest is the One I want to follow the rest of my life."

PRAYER

Praise God that He caused Peng's garden to bear well—
without a sacrifice to the spirits. Pray that Peng and other
Christians living in Communist controlled countries will
continue to hold strongly to their faith in the Lord. Pray
that God will send someone to translate the Word into
Peng's language.

MEDITATION

The heavens declare the glory of God; the skies proclaim
the work of his hands. Day after day they pour forth
speech; night after night they display knowledge. There
is no speech or language where their voice is not heard.
(Psalm 19:1–3)

You have heard me teach many things . . . Teach these
truths to trustworthy people who are able to pass them
on to others. (2 Timothy 2:2, NLT)

REFLECTION

Peng searched for God because he felt someone created
all he saw around him. And missionaries went to his
country to teach him the way of salvation through
Christ. Am I willing to have God send me overseas as
a missionary? If He doesn't send me, am I committed
to pray and give so others like Peng may find the One

38

who sends sunshine and rain, and liberates from the "strings" of the evil spirits?

---

[1]This story is gleaned from Rosemary Watson's book *All One Family*, Hudson Press, 7/600 North Road, Ormond, Vic 3204, copyright 2001, OMF International. A full account of Peng's story is told in Rosemary's book *As the Rock Flower Blooms*, Overseas Missionary Fellowship Ltd., 2 Cluny Road, Singapore 1025, Republic of Singapore (now out of print).

3

"I Have a Terrific Testimony!"

From infancy you have known the holy Scriptures, which are able to make you wise for salvation through faith in Christ Jesus.
— the apostle Paul, 2 Timothy 3:15

"The last three weeks, the gals at Bible study have been giving their testimonies," Karen[1] reported to her husband. "Peggy[2] told how she was shunted from foster home to foster home after her parents divorced. When she was fifteen, she ran away from her sixth home, then got into drugs and alcohol. In her last year of high school, a friend told her how much Jesus loved her, and she asked Him to come into her life and free her.

"Terri's first marriage—she was still in her teens—didn't last. After her divorce, she got pregnant and had an abortion. A neighbor lady led her to Jesus."

"Hmmm," Lyle grunted, letting her know he was still with her.

"Betsy—she's the intellectual one—is a lawyer and was skeptical about spiritual things. Some of the women where she worked invited her to a Bible study. She decided she'd go and prove to them that the Bible was wrong. 'But,' she said, 'my plan backfired. God's Word proved to me that I was the one who was wrong.' "

Another "Hmmm" from Lyle.

"All three of them have terrific testimonies," Karen continued. Then in a flat voice she added, "Next week I give my testimony."

"Karen," Lyle said with a mischievous twinkle in his eyes, "what you'd like is to have one of those 'terrific testimonies' without having to go through the agony those ladies went through, right?"

"Yeah, I guess you're right," Karen admitted, amazed as always at her husband's insight into her feelings.

Karen handed Lyle another slice of her freshly baked bread. "You know, I once overheard Mom tell a friend, 'When Karen was a teenager, she just had to rebel against something. So she continually moaned and groaned about having to eat the whole wheat bread that I baked each week.' "

She picked up a slice of the bread and waved it at Lyle, saying, "Can you imagine anyone rebelling at having to eat this?"

"Nope," Lyle replied, as he crammed in more of his wife's bread, baked using his mother-in-law's recipe.

Karen grew pensive. "But what was my rebellion compared to Peggy's and Terri's? Or Betsy's?"

Then, as though practicing for next week, she began, "All right girls, listen to my terrific testimony. Raised in a Christian home. Taught the Bible by Dad and Mom from day one of my birth. Accepted Jesus when I was five. Threw some fits in the next few years, as normal kids do. Then in my teen years, rebelled big time against my parents . . ." She grinned before adding "by getting fixes on white bread behind their backs and reading books late at night when I was supposed to be sleeping. But, in college chemistry, after learning that white bread won't even support mold growth, repented. A gradual growth in my Christian life through college and graduate school . . . and here I am today."

Before Lyle had a chance to comment on her syllogism, Karen lamented, "Just doesn't sound too exciting, does it?"

"Karen, maybe you could look at it this way: God saved you *from*—rather than *out of*—those things your friends went through."

Now it was Karen's turn to "Hmmm." But it was more than just letting her husband know she was with him; she was doing some deep thinking.

The next Thursday at Bible study, Karen began, "Last week I went home thinking about the terrific testimonies Peggy, Terri and Betsy have given. I know we all rejoice at what God did in their lives. I'm sure they would be the first to admit that it was God's grace—His 'unmerited favor,' as the theologians define it. In the second chapter of Ephesians, Paul tells us that it's by grace that we're saved . . .

"I also went home thinking my testimony is nothing when compared with theirs. But my husband made me see that my story is no less exciting, no less a testimony of God's grace. My parents were missionaries. I'm grateful that they faithfully taught me the

Word of God, and that I came to know Jesus at five years of age. Dedicated teachers in the mission schools helped ground me in the Christian faith. I realize that God saved me *from*—rather than *out of . . .*"

Karen paused. *What exactly did God save me from? If I had not been born in a Christian home, had not come to know Jesus when so young, my rebellious nature would certainly have manifested itself in many more ways.*

"Well," she continued, "thankfully, I'll never know just what He did save me from. But by His grace, that same grace that worked in each of our lives, He saved me—and that's exciting! I do have a terrific testimony. I'll never again get caught in the trap of thinking that others have a terrific testimony, but I don't. My testimony is of God's grace, just as Peggy's, Terri's and Betsy's testimonies are."

PRAYER
Lord, thank you, that in your grace, you have given me what I don't deserve. And by your mercy, you have not given me what I do deserve.

MEDITATION
You have been taught the holy Scriptures from childhood, and they have given you the wisdom to receive the salvation that comes by trusting in Christ Jesus. (2 Timothy 3:15, NLT)

For it is by grace you have been saved, through faith— and this not from yourselves, it is the gift of God—not by works, so that no one can boast. (Ephesians 2:8–9)

REFLECTION
Do I realize the propensity I have to sin and the depth of God's grace in saving me?

---

[1]Karen Loving Branagan is the daughter of Ed and Aretta Loving. Having grown up in Papua New Guinea, Karen developed an interest in missions, and she and her husband, Lyle, give generously to several missionaries. Lyle is an elder in their Associate Reformed Presbyterian Church, which supports a Wycliffe missionary family.

[2]Peggy, as well as Terri and Betsy, are pseudonyms.

It's Like Eating Ice Cream

4

Delight yourself also in the Lord and He shall give you the desires of your heart.

— **King David (Psalm 37:4, NKJV)**

"This job is like eating ice cream and being paid to eat it, even though our 'partners' actually support our ministry."

Both Tom and Irene feel the same way about their jobs. Loaned to Wycliffe by Christians in Action (CinA) Missions, the Hodges arrived in Waxhaw, N.C., at the JAARS Center in 1998. Not "new kids on the missions block" by any means, they had spent 14 years overseas, then 17 years at CinA headquarters in California. There Tom was the sole computer programmer for over 11 years, and Irene worked in accounting.

Irene's "like eating ice cream" job refers to keyboarding Scripture in languages from around the world, sent to her by Wycliffe Associates UK.[1] She has begun her 29th project—the Themne New Testament from Sierra Leone, W. Africa.

A few months ago, Irene wrote to those who partner with them in their ministry: "After typing chapters in the Azumenia language of Chad, I'm now working on S. Tiwa (Pueblo Indians). Join me in praying for these people."

Tom says, "Some people would call our coming to JAARS Center as 'having a call from God.' I call it fulfilling God's dream for our lives—one that took 12 years to become a reality."

In the mid-1980s, the Hodges were at a missions conference where Wycliffe translator Bob Weber displayed a paper at his table about the CADA[2] program. "I was amazed at how computers could help in translation," Tom says. "That day, a dream was born to use my computer skills to help speed up Bible translation." But the path to fulfilling that dream was closed. CinA had no replacement for him.

Tom describes himself as the "Biblical Caleb/Give me this mountain!" type. He began teaching himself linguistics. He went to night school to learn spreadsheets, databases, and programming a PC, which he says was "very different from the System/34 used at my job at our mission." He bought a PC and taught himself the "C" programming language. As a fun hobby, for two years he studied neural networks, which are used in analyzing speech.

"Was I discouraged sometimes? Yes," Tom says. "My dream turned four years old, and I was ready to give up, but God wasn't. We went to a Wycliffe Associates[3] banquet and the main speaker, some might say, 'just happened' to sit at our table. We knew God had placed him there. He encouraged us to press on."

Four years later, Tom was ready to give up again. Then, he attended another Wycliffe Associates banquet. "The wife of the translator who had encouraged us four years before 'just happened' to take the only seat left at our table. She too encouraged me to not give up on my, by now, eight-year-old dream."

Yet, by age 62, Tom's dream was fading into just enjoying studying linguistics and neural networks, and eventually retiring to a rocking chair there in California. Then a phone call revived his dream. It was from a Sunday School teacher he had known 25 years before. "We've driven from the east coast vacationing," said the caller. "We'll be at your house in two hours."

"That evening, as I talked of my dream and described my studies, my enthusiasm caused my visitor to challenge me to 'go for it,' " Tom says. "Not long afterwards, our mission replaced the System/34. I was no longer needed . . ."

Now they were free, and they decided to follow the advice of their East coast visitor and "go for it." But they faced obstacles, the biggest of which was dwindling support. "We were barely squeaking by, even with help from the mission and Irene's paycheck. At her job—typing yearbooks—she had to learn dozens of codes. Little did she know that learning and formatting those codes was preparing her for keyboarding Scripture at JAARS, where she uses linguistic and phonetic codes."

As they "went for it," Tom and Irene felt overwhelmed by the support issue. But studying Henry Blackaby's *Experiencing God* challenged them that real faith requires one to step out into the void. "The turning point came when we realized we had to leave behind financial help from our mission," Tom says. "We did, and God began to not only meet our needs, but also called some of the greatest people in the world to pray for and support our ministry."

Another obstacle was the sale of their house, which was on the market for months. At a men's breakfast, Tom asked for prayer. One of the men there actually knew someone who had applied for a loan—to buy Tom and Irene's house! "My wife is a realtor and can handle it for you," he offered. Handle it, she did! She closed escrow in about two weeks.

"It didn't hit us that we were actually going to JAARS until the huge, 60-foot-long JAARS tractor-trailer rolled up to load our things," Tom says.

After the tractor-trailer left, they sank to the bare floor. "Are we dead yet?" The humor of an exhausted Irene brought the medicine of laughter to their weary minds and bodies.

The evening before they left, Irene read Psalm 132:6b in her New Living Translation, "We found it in the distant countryside of Jaar." Though "it" refers to the Ark of the Covenant, they thought of JAARS "in the distant countryside of" North Carolina!

At sunset, Tom saw an unusual cloud formation, which he describes as "a hand on the eastern horizon with three enormous fingers. One reached from the eastern horizon to just over my head, one towards the north, one towards the south. We took this as the Lord saying, 'Come this way to JAARS. Your path is now open.' "

They arrived at the Center in June 1998, the 50th anniversary year of JAARS. "Emerging from the forested road, the first thing we saw was the Language Services Center building, under construction. A huge banner on the building read, LOOK WHAT GOD IS DOING! We echoed, LOOK WHAT GOD HAS DONE these last twelve years to get us here!"

Do Tom and Irene have any regrets about leaving California to serve with JAARS?

"Well," Tom says, "my long-time, after-hours study of neural networks for speech analysis as a fun hobby was hardly used after I arrived at JAARS. Though I was somewhat disappointed about that at first, during several years as a research assistant, I got to teach myself other interesting technologies. I've endeavored to serve cheerfully wherever I'm needed. And I've had a lot of fun doing that!"

And Irene says, "Who would regret eating ice cream and feeling you were being paid to eat it?"

Tom concludes that "No one is too young or too old to receive and fulfill a dream from God when we delight ourselves in Him."

PRAYER

Pray with Irene for those who will read the Scriptures she keyboards. Pray for God to lead more people with computer expertise to work in the JAARS Information Technology (IT) department. Praise God that Tom, at age 71, is enjoying life serving the Lord in JAARS IT.

MEDITATION

The best that people can do is eat, drink, and enjoy their work. I saw that even this comes from God, because no one can eat or enjoy life without him. (Ecclesiastes 2:24-25, NCV)

How thankful I am to Christ Jesus our Lord for . . . appointing me to serve him. (I Timothy 1:12, NLT)

REFLECTION

Tom says, "Though not an exact quote, the thought on a Norman Nelson tape was, 'Your dream to serve the Lord may be God dreaming His dream through you. If so, He will bring it to pass—in His time.' " Do I really believe God can give me a job that both He and I delight in, as He did for Tom and Irene?

[1]Although Wycliffe Associates UK primarily serves Wycliffe Bible Translators, they cooperate with the Bible Societies and other mission organizations (including WEC and OM). A team of over 400 people keyboard Scripture, both newly translated and books where no computer files are available. The latter is important for those who need to revise and reprint Scripture published before the days computers were used in Bible translation.

[2]CADA (Computer Assisted Dialect Adaptation) assisted in translation from one language dialect to another. It has since been replaced by CARLA (Computer Assisted Related Language Adaptation). CARLA is especially helpful when there are several languages in the same family. A translator can use this program to more quickly do a translation into one of those other, related languages.

[3]Wycliffe Associates USA was founded in 1960 to support Wycliffe Bible Translators in practical, tangible ways. They recruit and mobilize laypeople who volunteer their "time, talents, and treasure" in ministry to accelerate the work of Bible translation.

5

Son of Hope

By grace you have been saved! We do not read it in Kant or Schopenhauer, or in any book of natural or secular history, and certainly not in any novel, but in the Bible alone.

— Karl Barth

Maximum security prisons—his home for almost thirty years! Sentenced to over 300 years, David Berkowitz is now serving the first of six consecutive life terms. "I sought demonic entities to communicate with and in turn, received power from them," he says. "As a servant of Satan, I took innocent lives. Now I deeply regret my actions."

David realizes he not only destroyed lives of others, he also threw away many years of his own life. "I would do anything to go back in time and change things. But such opportunities only happen in movies. I deserve my sentence. Even more, I deserve death."

In 1977 David was apprehended for his yearlong crime spree. "A platoon of police officers surrounded my car. Guns pointed at me from every direction. One sudden move and I would have been blasted into eternity."

Two years later in the infamous Attica prison, an inmate slit David's throat with a razor blade. "The prison doctor declared it a miracle that my jugular vein wasn't severed." David states the grim fact: "If I had died then, I'd be in hell today."

David tried hard to adjust to prison life, but battled depression, fed by anger. He began to think, *What do I have to live for?* Despair and loneliness stalked him as he had stalked his victims on the streets of New York City. "I began to think about ending my life," he says.

Then one cold December night in 1987 when he was walking in the prison yard, an inmate from another cellblock approached him. *I don't know this guy, he doesn't know me. What's his line?* David wondered. The unwritten convict code dictates you don't speak to a stranger. For security reasons, prisoners stay in their own cliques.

"Hi! I'm Rick. And you're David Berkowitz," the stranger stated.

Past attacks had programmed caution in David. "Yeah, so what?"

"God sent me here to tell you that He loves you and has a plan for your life," Rick said.

"I laughed at the guy. 'You're wrong, man,' I told him. No way could God love me. I'm too evil. You're wasting time talking to me about God.' But Rick wore a big smile and held a little book in his hand. Even though I instantly rejected what he said, he had a compassionate attitude that drew me to him."

Over the weeks as Rick persevered, he and David became friends. As they walked and talked, Rick's main theme was always God's infinite love and mercy, available for everyone. Still, David continued to feel he was too evil for God to love. And David had another reason for rejecting Rick's message: "I'm Jewish."

From that "little book," Rick explained, "Romans 3:23 says all have sinned. We've all failed to glorify God. Jews and non-Jews, we all need a Savior. And God loves each of us. That's why He sent Jesus—the One your people call Yeshua—to be our Savior."

One day Rick presented David with a gift: a little book, just like the one he carried—a Gideon New Testament with Psalms. "God has a special word for you in the Psalms."

Late at night, David would randomly choose a Psalm. "I'd never read the Bible before. The words were the most beautiful I'd ever heard. It seemed as though God was talking directly to me. I identified with King David as he poured out his pain to God."

Several weeks later, close to midnight—as David says, "It happened." He read: "This poor man cried, and the Lord heard him, and saved him out of all his troubles" (Psalm 34:6, KJV). "Those words pierced deep within. Guilt, anger, shame, feelings of failure, loneliness, hurt—they all hit me at once."

He turned out his cell light, and in darkness he wept. "I threw myself down on my knees and cried out to God, 'I'm sorry for the evil things I've done. Forgive me!' I felt He was right there beside me. I got up, at peace for the first time in my thirty-three years."

Two days later in the prison yard he told Rick what had happened. "Praise God!" Rick shouted. "You've been born again. Read about it in chapter three of John's Gospel. You're a new person in Christ."

Reflecting on that experience, David says, "God began breaking Satan's chains of oppression and torment that had bound me for many long, ugly years. Now years have passed since God sent that prisoner with a big smile and a little New Testament into my life. He introduced me to Jesus. Old things left my life and new things entered—just as 2 Corinthians 5:17 in the Bible says. Today, through God's grace, I serve Jesus here in prison. I no longer see being here as punishment. Yes, doing time is difficult. But I try to see myself as a missionary serving in a distant land. There's a ripe harvest of hungry hearts in this prison and this is my mission field," David says.

"I also see my imprisonment as a training ground to help me become a more mature believer and a man of strong faith. I no longer identify with the evil 'Son of Sam,'[1] a name that represents demons and death, a name I'm now ashamed of. God has given me a new name—'Son of Hope.'

"I feel freer in prison than I ever felt my entire life, because I know Jesus Christ. What more can I say but Thank you, Jesus!" he says with a smile. And when David smiles, you can't help but see the joy and peace of Jesus in his face.

As David serves God in his official job at the prison's Mental Health Unit, he counsels and encourages emotionally challenged peers, many as depressed and tormented as he once was. Besides his daytime ministry, at night David prays for his country and the nations of the world; for the people he writes to, many of them missionaries; for viewers of *The Choice is Yours*.[2]

PRAYER

Praise God that no darkness of the soul is so dense that the light of God's Word can't penetrate it; no depression of the spirit so deep that the hammer of God's Word can't reach down and smash it; no chain binding the will so strong that the Sword of the Spirit can't cut it in pieces. God's mercy is unlimited! Thank God for The Gideons and other organizations that distribute God's Word. Ask God to anoint David with His Holy Spirit as he serves Him in prison.

MEDITATION

Christ Jesus came into the world to save sinners—of whom I am the worst. But for that very reason I was shown mercy so that in me . . . Christ Jesus might display his unlimited patience . . . (1 Timothy 1:15–16)

And everyone who calls on the name of the Lord will be saved." (Joel 2:32)

REFLECTION

Am I tempted to think that it's not fair that someone as evil as David (or the apostle Paul) should receive forgiveness? If so, maybe it shows how little I understand God's grace and mercy. Could it be I've not comprehended that my sin sent Jesus to the cross? Will

Campbell, struggling to come to terms with the brutal murder of his best friend by a serial murderer, wrote in *Brother to a Dragonfly:* "That God would set him free is almost more than I could stand. But unless that is precisely the case . . . there is no Gospel, there is no Good News. Unless that is the truth, we have only bad news."

---

[1] "Son of Sam" marked David as a soldier of Samhain, ancient Celtic god of the dead and a high ranking prince of Satan. Druid priests celebrated the eve of the Celtic New Year, October 31st, shedding animal and human blood to appease Samhain.

[2] *The Choice is Yours,* a video of David's testimony, targets young people, warning of drugs, alcohol and violence. Gospel Communications distributes it. You may order at www.GospelDirect.com or phone 1-800-Gospel Direct (1-800-467-7353).

6

Sharpening the Axe

By translating the Bible, the Djambarrpuyngu men and women are taking God into their culture and demonstrating that He is not just a "whitefella's" God. He is their God and He speaks their language.
—Rebecca Hayman

Wielding a newly sharpened axe, Maratja and a team of women take turns chopping until the tree falls apart, exposing a hollowed inside flowing with *guku* (wild honey). They step back as dozens of small fingers quickly reach in to scoop up the sticky sweetness. As the last of the *guku* drips off fingers and chins, the children are admonished, "Listen and don't forget. God's Word is much sweeter than wild honey!"

Maratja—and the team of choppers—live in northern Australia. All help translate the Bible for their people, the Djambarrpuyngu of Arnhem Land. Marks of that translation project have been:

Discouragement—but also perseverance. Di Buchanan, with the Uniting Church,[1] began the project in 1976. After she passed away, Wanymuli, the woman who worked with her, continued translating.

Dedication. "This work has become like my close relative," Wanymuli says. "God pointed out this work to me and touched my heart. I will never run away from His work." That the project didn't fold can be attributed to dedicated servants of God, such as this woman, and also to the backing of the Uniting Church.

Difficulties. Rebecca Hayman, former editor of the Wycliffe Australia magazine, *Beyond Words*,[2] says, "To take a story about an ancient agrarian society and secure it in the language of a people who are hunters and gatherers is extremely difficult. It requires a huge cultural as well as linguistic leap. Many words in the Bible are completely alien to Djambarrpuyngu culture. For instance, *king* and *slave*. And abstract concepts such as *grace, mercy, forgiveness, sacrifice.* Translators struggle to express God's Word in the heart language. They must delve into the depths of the Gospel and they cannot help but be moved by it."

Delight. "Newly translated Scripture cuts into our innermost parts and judges our thoughts and attitudes; sometimes it brings tears of joy," says Gapany, one of the women on the team, affirming that indeed the team members are moved by the Word as they translate it.

Diligence. Maratja says, "If Aboriginal people are to survive as a race, they must have God's Word. We face pressure from both inside and outside our communities. Yes," he reiterates, "we must have God's Word!"

Determination. Showing their resolve to get the Word to their people, eight Djambarrpuyngus finished 475 hours of translation training in a government accredited course designed by SIL to train mother-tongue translators.

And more Delight! Yurranydjil, one of those who finished the training, described learning translation techniques as "sharpening the axe so we can cut for the sweetest honey." The others nodded. They too have tasted forest *guku*. And as they translate, they taste that "The ordinances of the Lord are . . . sweeter than honey, than honey from the comb" (Psalm 19:9, 10).[3]

Epilogue
Margaret Miller, with the Uniting Church, has worked with the Djambarrpuyngu team in the last few years. Today Maratja and Djawut along with the women on the team—Gapany, Maatjarra, Ngandama, Waangarr, Wanymuli, Yurranydjil and Margaret—anticipate that the New Testament will be published by The Bible Society of Indonesia, and later this year dedicated in Arnhem land, Australia.

PRAYER

Pray for Margaret and those on the Djambarrpuyngu team (even if you can't pronounce their names or the name of their language!) to remain faithful in all aspects of their lives. Pray for good health for them and their families. Pray that the Djambarrpuyngu people will read God's Word.

MEDITATION

How sweet are Your words to my taste, sweeter than honey to my mouth! (Psalm 119:103)

REFLECTION

How much do I treasure God's Word? How often do I claim that "I don't have time to read the Word" and yet find time to eat?

---

[1]Today the Djambarrpuyngu translation team works under the auspices of the Uniting Church and receives assistance from consultants with The Bible Society in Australia and from AUSIL (Australian Society of Indigenous Languaages) in Darwin, Australia.

[2]*Beyond Words* is produced three times a year by Wycliffe Australia. Visit the Wycliffe Australia Web site (see Appendix A) to view a selection of articles or to subscribe.

[3]"Sharpening the Axe" was translated into Dutch by Wycliffe Netherlands and published in a small book called *Zoeter dan Honing*, 2002.

7
A Living-Walking Translation

The sacred Scriptures are the property of the people. Through doing the things contained in this book we may all together come to the everlasting life.
—**John Wycliffe**

"Is your religion a different kind of Christianity? We believe in God, and we're Christians. But we've been told the Bible is not for us; it's for ordained church workers only. We were warned that if we read it, a curse might fall on us."

That's how some of the Paranan people of the Philippines expressed their concerns. But they brought their concerns to the right person: Tereza Chiong, working with Translators Association of the Philippines (TAP).[1] "As I and the team of Paranan men and women continued translating God's Word, they saw that no curse fell on us. Instead, they saw people full of peace and joy," Tereza testifies.

"Translation is one of the best tools in evangelism and even the birth of churches. As we translate and as we do comprehension checks—that is, read the translated Scripture to people to see if they understand it—people often come to know Jesus."

After Arnold Alverez accepted the Lord, he gave up his job and obeyed God's calling to serve his people, telling them the Bible is for *them* too. Arnold now pastors the first believers' church in Palanan.[2] And he is finishing the translation of the New Testament—a work Ramon and Tereza could not continue because God led them to another ministry and because of Ramon's health. "Despite persecution from loved ones, Arnold has not turned back," Tereza says.

A few years ago, a powerful typhoon hit the Palanan area, leaving many people homeless and destroying their crops. "Despite this test, the believers didn't give up their faith. Instead, they were drawn closer to God," Tereza says.

Today Paranan churches commission and send out workers to other areas. "Looking back on my 20 years of working with these people, I see how God moves when His Word is read in the language people can understand best," Tereza says. "From zero believers, a total of eight churches and a fellowship in each of the 17 *baranggays* (town subdivisions) now exist. It happened because we lived in a village with the people, learned their language, and adapted to their culture. Bible translation becomes dynamic when the translator's life is a living-walking translation of God's love."

PRAYER

Praise God for what He has done among the Paranan, and pray for the Christians in their efforts to lead people to Jesus. Pray that Tereza's life will continue to be a living-walking translation of God's Word in her new role as coordinator of TAP's Member Care Department. Pray for Arnold Alvarez, and Moni Chiong as he supervises the Palanan translation and works with those translating the Old Testament into Palanan Agta, a related language.

MEDITATION

How, then, can they call on the one they have not believed in? And how can they believe in the one of whom they have not heard? And how can they hear without someone preaching to them? (Romans 10:14)

And whatever you do, whether in word or deed, do it all in the name of the Lord Jesus, giving thanks to God the Father through him. (Colossians 3:17)

REFLECTION

Is my life a living-walking translation of God's Word to those I live among?

---

[1]TAP was formed in 1983 to complement and eventually finish the work begun over 50 years ago in the Philippines by Wycliffe. Ted Abadiano served as TAP's first executive director, followed by Tony Dasalla, then Helen Madrid. Today Boi Awid fills that position. TAP personnel are involved in 17 language projects. Literacy, health and other community development work is also part of their work. Plans are underway to survey the remaining languages of the Philippines, then place translation teams where needs exist, thus helping fulfill Vision 2025. To further help fulfill that vision, The Alliance Graduate School (Christian and Missionary Alliance), TAP and SIL cooperate in a "Joint Academic Program" offering training in Bible translation and linguistics. The one-year program confers the Graduate Diploma in Applied Linguistics. To order an informational video, e-mail tap@ i-manila.com.ph or TAP@sil.org, or write TAP Office, Quezon City, 931-3087.

[2]Although the people are called *Paranan*, the language and the area is known as *Palanan*.

8

A People with an
Endless Hope

Whenever and wherever God's Word comes to a people in their own language, it changes lives and person by person it changes the world.
— **Bernie May, Founder and former CEO of The Seed Company**[1]

"A people without hope."

That's how Bernie May, former JAARS pilot, at one time described the Machiguenga people of Peru. Through the years, Bernie flew Wycliffe translators Wayne and Betty Snell to Machiguenga land. The Machiguengas lived in small encampments scattered over several hundred square miles of rainforest near the headwaters of the Amazon.

"The challenge," Betty says, "was how to reach the several thousand Machiguenga people with the Scriptures, as well as with education and medical help. Because of their isolation there were no schools among them."

The Snells settled in at a workstation where a Spanish businessman employed Machiguengas. With the help of those men and their families, they began to learn and analyze the complicated Machiguenga language. After constructing an alphabet, they taught a few to read their language. At first, *What purpose could learning to read possibly serve?* was the attitude of these uninfluenced-by-the-outside-world people. But gradually they developed a love for learning new things, and their attitude changed to, *This is fun and exciting!*

Eventually, villages were formed and schools established. "As soon as some Machiguengas believed God's message, they wanted all their people to hear. Men paddled up tributaries looking for other Machiguengas," the Snells say.

The New Testament, translated by the Snells and a team of Machiguengas and published by Bible League, was dedicated in early 1997. A Machiguenga couple, Angel and Olga Diaz, have been appointed by the church as translators for the Nanti, a neighboring group.

"At the time the Snells went to live with the Machiguenga people, this no-hope group was classified as an 'unreached people group.' They now are a people with a heavenly hope, a people with a vision to reach out to others who have no hope," Bernie says. "And we in Wycliffe, through The Seed Company, partnered with the Machiguenga church to take the Gospel to their neighbors. 'The Lord has prospered me, and I can help those people,' a businessman in Virginia offered. 'I will pray every day,' a student in Chicago volunteered. That man gave money. That student gave time in prayer. People like them, partnering with The Seed

Company and a people group, form an unbeatable team!"

Translators and consultants, SAMair and pilots trained at JAARS, dedicated laypeople who pray and give joined with a language group changed by the translated Word. Indeed, an unbeatable team! And all on that team know they are "people with an endless hope, not a hopeless end."

PRAYER

Praise God for The Seed Company. Praise Him for the commitment of Angel and Olga Diaz. Pray for them as they continue to adapt Machiguenga Scriptures into the Nanti language. Pray that God will protect the Diazes and the Nanti communities. Ask Him to give peaceful contacts with isolated pockets of Nanti people still potentially hostile to factions of their own people as well as to outsiders. Pray that God will continue to cause many Nanti people to respond to His Word.

MEDITATION

You will receive power when the Holy Spirit comes on you; and you will be my witnesses in Jerusalem, and in all Judea and Samaria, and to the ends of the earth. (Acts 1:8)

The Lord announced the word, and great was the company of those who proclaimed it. (Psalm 68:11)

REFLECTION

In her poem "Lift the Veil," Rosemary Watson prays:

Awaken my mind and soul, Lord,
To receive the great truths of your Word.
Give me your love and your passion
To share the Good News I have heard.

Are people you work with or people who live across the street from you "a people with no hope"? Are you seeking to share the Good News with others, as the Machiguengas are with their neighbors?

---

[1]"Creatively networking with God's people around the world to translate the Bible into every language for His glory—that's our vision," says Roy Peterson, CEO of The Seed Company. "To fulfill our vision, we support local personnel translating their own Scriptures."

9

ASL? LSQ?
Does It Make a Difference?

Through deaf people, God has created signed languages with rich potential for expressing the truths in His Word, in some ways better than in spoken languages.

— **Albert Bickford, Wycliffe**

To the uninitiated, it would have appeared Diane Campbell[1] was embarking on a long and elaborate holiday. But in fact, 300 *Life of Christ* American Sign Language (ASL) videos[2] filled most of her suitcases. She hoped to distribute these on the eastern coast of Canada.

Diane's five-month assignment was to conduct a sign language survey for the North America Branch of SIL. "In Canada there are four different sign languages," she was told. She would confirm or refute that "fact," as well as determine how many of these languages needed a separate translation. Would people sign, "Yes, thank you! I want an ASL video"? Or would the Deaf in Canada not know ASL, and therefore refuse the video?

"Interviews and more interviews. Pages and pages of data collection. All with the view toward analyzing the situation to find an answer to the question: Will the Deaf in Canada need their own separate sign language translation?" Diane says.

Some—those who knew ASL—accepted the free videos. Others, whose language was LSQ (Quebec Sign Language), turned away because "These aren't in our language."

"I rejoiced that some people took videos, but I was disappointed that ASL could not clearly communicate the Gospel to these LSQ signers," Diane says. "That showed us that ASL was not their heart language. And the purpose of the survey, after all, was to determine if a Deaf translation project was needed in Canada. Their refusal of the videos proved that, yes, these people really did need an LSQ translation."

Diane herself is hearing impaired, so she's especially sensitive to communication issues that deaf people face. "The Deaf often don't understand the host country language. Usually it's a second language for them. That's why the host country language, in this case spoken English or spoken French, doesn't adequately communicate the Gospel to these LSQ signers." That's the bad news. The good news is that translation is going on through several different organizations in over 23 sign languages worldwide.[3]

PRAYER

Praise God for the successful survey in Canada. Pray for Diane as she continues to conduct surveys among the Deaf. Pray that the Lord of the harvest will send more translators to work with the Deaf.

MEDITATION

People were overwhelmed with amazement. "He [Jesus] has done everything well," they said. "He even makes the deaf hear . . . " (Mark 7:37)

"Everyone who calls on the name of the Lord will be saved." How, then, can they call on the one they have not believed in? And how can they believe in the one of whom they have not heard? And how can they hear without someone preaching [or signing] to them [in a sign language they understand]? (Romans 10:13–14)

REFLECTION

How much do I understand about problems the Deaf have in "hearing" God's Word? For instance, a video Bible is extremely expensive to produce. If there is a complete video Bible in an understandable sign language, the average deaf person cannot afford to buy it. And that deaf person certainly could not carry all those videos to church.

---

[1]For security reasons, a pseudonym has been used.

[2]In 1980, Deaf Missions of Council Bluffs, Iowa, initiated the ASL translation project, first producing the ASL *Life of Christ* videos. The Scripture Sign Project, organized by an Assembly of God Church in New York and directed by Jeanne Bricker, supplied Diane with the ASL videos. Deaf Missions aims to put a free copy of the *Life of Christ* video in the hands of every deaf person in America.

[3]Albert Bickford, director of the SIL linguistic school at the University of North Dakota, says, "Based on what we know now, I anticipate that at least 150 sign languages will need Bible translation work."

10

And They Listened

I've been overwhelmed by God's grace and power as I've read of the entrance of understanding and light in lives once characterized by darkness. And it's all by the powerful influence of the Truth whether in printed form, audio, video, oral or film.

— Dick Elkins, Wycliffe

Pastor Dhana Raj[1] hung his head as his neighbors mocked him. "We can't hear our TVs. Shut up!" Listening to television rated higher on their scale of values than listening to the young pastor preach God's Word.

Despite ridicule and scorn, each day his voice went out over the loudspeaker. Loud and clear, he could be heard by any who wanted to listen. But sadly, none did. After months of trying, Pastor Raj told God, "I've done all I can. That's it, I guess. I can't reach these people."

Then a missionary friend stopped by to visit. After listening to the disheartened pastor tell of his attempts to give his neighbors the Gospel, his friend said, "I have good news for you." He then told him about Hosanna and its Faith Comes by Hearing (FCBH) program. "The New Testament has been recorded on cassette tapes in Telegu—the language your neighbors spoke in their homes as children, their heart language."

"I'm not sure anything could turn these people toward God," the disheartened pastor replied. Nevertheless, he reluctantly agreed to meet with an FCBH worker.

"He'll give you a set of Bible tapes and show you how to use them," his friend promised.

One evening soon afterwards, silence reigned in the village. No blaring TVs, no crying children . . . That silence, created by a power outage, gave Pastor Raj the opportunity to broadcast the first FCBH tape over his loudspeaker. Hesitantly, he placed the cassette into a battery-operated recorder and hit the play button. *Will they listen? Or will they yell at me again?*

After several minutes, not hearing any sound at all from his neighbors, the timid pastor peeked out the church door. He saw people standing in their doorways. *They're listening! Thank you, Lord!* No mocking, no complaining—just silent people, listening intently to God's Word.

After an hour, Pastor Raj turned off the tape recorder and watched as people walked toward the church. "That was our language! God was speaking to us through those tapes. We should have listened to you before," a spokesman for the group confessed. Some began asking questions about what they had heard.

A no-longer-timid pastor, with joy spilling over his face and into his eyes, reports, "My people weren't interested in God's Word preached in a language that wasn't their mother tongue. But when they heard a Bible tape[2] that spoke their language, they listened. Then after I answered their questions, instead of mocking me, they lined up, waiting to receive Jesus as their Lord and Savior!"

PRAYER

Thank you, Father, that Hosanna records and distributes your Word in audio. Pray that the over 900 million people in India will have opportunity to hear God's Word. Pray for Indian pastors as they seek to share His Word in audio. Pray that people who won't—or can't—read the Bible will have the opportunity to hear it.

MEDITATION

"Call them all together," the Lord instructed, "—men, women, children, and foreigners living among you—to hear the laws of God and to learn his will, so that you will reverence the Lord your God and obey his laws." (Deuteronomy 31:12, TLB)

REFLECTION

Have I considered and thanked God that His Word is available to me in so many different forms: written, audiocassette, video, DVD, radio? What I am doing to ensure that others hear it?

---

[1]Dhana Raj is a pseudonym.

[2]Pastor Raj's village is just one of over one thousand villages that Hosanna's FCBH program has reached. See Appendix B for a fuller account of Hosanna's Ministry.

11

They Dance by the Light of the Moon

Translating Scripture gives the words. Technology makes it possible to record those words onto cassettes and CDs. Recorded Scripture songs in the heart language of a people are a powerful communication tool.
—Dan Bauman, Wycliffe

"It's like the old days when we were children! Young people used to play music under the light of the moon to entertain the old folks."

On hearing such comments from many older people, Pastor Josias Djenné responded with, "Yes, these new Bissa songs have encouraged us. In our church, some don't understand the foreign songs, especially the older people. But when we sing Bissa songs and beat the calabash,[1] even the old people come to church. And they understand God is alive because they listen to the music."

For many years, Pastor Djenné had desired to see his Bissa people of Burkina Faso, West Africa, reached with the message of God's Word. "I was especially concerned for the elderly," he says. "Now this new kind of music is impacting our whole community."

Delighted with these under-the-light-of-the-moon evening "concerts," this Assembly of God pastor's voice reflected almost childlike enthusiasm.

Along with men from four other churches in the Bissa area, Pastor Djenné had worked with Ruud and Connie Hidden of Wycliffe Netherlands to translate the Bissa New Testament. "Right from the beginning of the project in 1979, we cooperated with local government agencies to develop an alphabet and to set up a literacy program in Bissa," Ruud says.

Despite that literacy program, once the New Testament was published, a large segment of the Bissa population was unable to read it—mainly those "elderly" for whom Pastor Djenné was concerned. In 1998, as he held in his hands a computer-generated copy of the New Testament, he wondered, *How can we reach these older people? They rarely leave their homes.*

As he wondered, a young American lady became part of the solution to his "How can we?" dilemma. Mary Hendershott, a Wycliffe ethnomusicologist,[2] regularly holds music workshops with different language groups in Burkina Faso. And that year Mary held a music workshop with the Bissa people. Scripture songs using Bissa song styles set to traditional music were composed by workshop participants.

"Up until then," Mary says, "the Bissa church had used French hymns or music borrowed from a larger, nearby ethnic group. This new music not only uses the heart language of the Bissa people, it also uses their heart music. I was elated as I listened to Pastor Djenné's enthusiastic report on what has happened."

"Since that workshop," Pastor Djenné says, "our people now hear our own music—Bissa music—and they pour out to listen." Then with a broad smile and eyes alight, Pastor Djenné claims, "This music deeply touches the hearts of these elderly ones! They hear the message as well as the music."

And not just the elderly—Bissa people of all ages are excited about this "new thing" that has become a part of everyday life. "People sing these new songs in their homes," says Pastor Djenné. "As they work together in their fields or building houses, they sing them. They walk down the street singing them. People who haven't yet believed in Jesus hear and take note. Some now come to church just to hear the music."

Recently Mary returned to Bukino Faso and helped with another workshop. She was greeted with the news that "Many of our Bissa people have listened and come to the Lord." One person reported, "The people love these songs! When we drum the melodies with the calabash, people cannot just pass on by."

Someone else added, "One evening the chief and all the elders started dancing right out in the chief's courtyard. They wanted us to play the music all night long."

Pastor Djenné concludes, "This new way of worshipping is here to stay!"

Today Pastor Djenné preaches to his congregation from one of the 10,000 published Bissa New Testaments.[3] As he does, he notes, with praise to God, the number of elderly people there—because, as he says, "They listened to the music!"[4]

PRAYER

Praise God that a music workshop revived the Bissa traditional music, and now the Good News is proclaimed in song. Pray for Mary Hendershott as she holds other music workshops. Pray that the Bissa will read the translated Scripture and proclaim His love by their actions as well as in song.

MEDITATION

He put a new song in my mouth, a hymn of praise to our God. Many will see and fear and put their trust in the Lord. (Psalm 40:3)

Praise the Lord. Sing to the Lord a new song, his praise in the assembly of the saints ... Let them praise his name with dancing and make music to him with tambourine and harp. (Psalm 149:1,3)

REFLECTION

When did I last sing to the Lord as a part of my daily worship of Him?

____

[1] The calabash, a large gourd, is also called bottle gourd, or squash gourd. The calabash is cut in half, then dried and made into a musical instrument. It is turned upside down on the ground and tapped or beat on with the fists.

[2] Wycliffe has several full-time, as well as part-time, ethnomusicologists (those who study the music of a particular region and its sociocultural implications). Tom Avery, assisted by his wife Kristy, is Wycliffe's International Ethnomusicology Coordinator. Contact him at ethnomusicology@sil.org for information and opportunities for service.

[3] In 2000, the Bissa New Testament was typeset and sent away for publication. Church representatives signed a letter approving the translation and pledged to do all they could to facilitate its use in the churches. "That was a joyful moment for Pastor Djenné and for all of us," Ruud says. This New Testament, dedicated in early 2002, was a joint effort by Wycliffe and Comité de Traduction de la Bible en Bissa, a committee representing all the Bissa-speaking churches.

[4] This story appears in *All the World is Singing, Glorifying God through the Worship Music of the Nations*, Frank Fortunato with Paul Neeley and Carol Brinneman, 2006, Authentic Publishing, Tryone, GA.

12

How Shall They Hear?

God's Word is able to pass through any thick wall to find, reach, and transform.
— **M. J. Zani**[1]

Mystery and mystique. Centuries of deeply ingrained ritual and tradition. Sometimes a "No missionaries allowed!" policy. Nonliterate. Incarcerated. How then shall all people hear God's message of salvation and life?

How shall the people of the world's most populous country, China, hear? How shall believers there grow in faith when Bibles are often confiscated and meeting together is prohibited?

Since 1985, Trans World Radio (TWR) and several other international Gospel broadcasters have been committed to providing every person on earth an opportunity to hear the Gospel by radio. This "World by Radio" partnership seeks to produce and broadcast Christian programming to every megalanguage group (defined by TWR as languages understood by at least one million people). As part of that commitment, TWR has been instrumental in distributing almost 68,000 Radio Church Planting kits in China. People in small, clandestine fellowship groups often use the radio and the materials in those kits to study God's Word.

One Chinese believer wrote: "Let us give praise to God who gives clear weather and peaceful nights. Only on silent nights can the clear signal of a radio transmission travel across thousands of miles to reach us here."

Another wrote: "You have answered many of my difficult questions. My brothers and sisters here want to understand and be able to explain the Bible so we can bring people to Christ. Our churches, even our Bibles and hymnals, were taken from us. But thank God, the faith of most is still firm."

Nonbelievers also write in. An old man whose one grandfather was a minister, and the other a church elder, wrote that he had "walked through dark periods. For 40 years I have been a lost sheep. When I was 15 years old I left home and any chance to know God. I was involved in the Chinese Revolution. I have begged, been in prison, and served as an army officer. Now I'm retired. And though I attended university, I'm like a child who needs to know everything about the Lord from the beginning." He ends his letter with a plea: "I look to you for help."[2]

How shall people hear in countries where a dominant religion, often opposed to Christianity, reigns?

TWR receives letters from many such "sensitive" or "restricted" countries. From Myanmar comes this letter: "There are forty believers in our village. I thank the Lord for your program. Through it, we learn more about God's great love for us."

A woman in Malaysia wrote, "My friend became a believer. I would like to help her understand more about the Bible. Please send booklets for beginners in Christ for my friend and me."

A Nepalese army man wrote that he used to attend church, "But," he says, "I am not a Christian. Your broadcast is helping me know Jesus. I want to read the Bible now, but I don't have one."

Someone from Romania wrote, "I can't express the joy I have because of your ministry. I listen to both the Romanian and Gypsy programs. I'd like to have a Bible in the Romani language."[3]

From Punjab comes this: "Your Bible study helps me understand God's Word. My interest in the Bible is increasing."

How shall the many lonely prisoners hear the message of freedom in Christ? How shall they be nurtured in their faith?

Lonely. Outcast. Without purpose. This describes the life of many men and women who sit in jail cells day after day, year after year. Often, more than just prison walls surround these people. Some, imprisoned unjustly, fight to remain free from the bondage of bitterness. Some carry heavy sin-and-guilt loads. Many are incarcerated far from their families or homelands, and walls of isolation and despair close in on them. God's Word breaks through those walls and reaches through iron bars to bring hope to this captive audience. As they hear Gospel broadcasts, many are set free from their sin and loneliness.

In India, a man serving a life sentence for murder turned his small radio to a TWR station. Intrigued, day after day there in his small cell he listened. He wrote, "Jesus has made me new. If I wasn't here in prison, I never would have gotten up so early. And I wouldn't have heard about Jesus. So I'm thankful I'm in prison."

"Thanks to my Lord and Savior Jesus Christ," a man from the Czech Republic wrote. "His light penetrates this dark place. I share a cell with my brother, who a few weeks ago came to that 'new birth' we've heard about on your broadcasts. We have the joy of the Christ's presence, but we miss hearing spoken words from outside. Except for our prayers, your broadcasts provide our only communication. Explanations given on the Thru the Bible program are especially appreciated."

A man from Poland reports, "My parents were atheists. I never held a Bible, never heard a Christian radio program. When only 17, my gods—alcohol and money—saw to it that I landed in prison. I had an old radio and came across your Thru the Bible program. I began to listen and I've committed my life to Christ. Those programs put me on the right path." Now, released from prison, this man is married and holds a job.

How shall God's chosen people—the people of Israel—hear the truth that Yeshua is indeed their Messiah?

In late 1998, Israeli Messianic Jews joined with TWR and launched a radio broadcast from Central Asia called Kol HaYeshua (The Voice of Salvation). This was the first time a TWR Hebrew program was heard across the entire land of Israel—from Elat to Haifa, from Tel Aviv to Jerusalem.

After the first Kol HaYeshua program aired, listeners began to respond. The first to respond, a man from Tel Aviv, phoned and said, "Because I am blind, your program is the only way I hear about the Messiah. Be bold to speak more about Yeshua and His goodness to bring salvation to the people of Israel."

Listeners throughout Israel continue to express gratitude—at least most do. One missile, a Molotov cocktail, was hurled at a producer's home in Jerusalem. It failed to explode.

How shall they hear? Real hearing takes place when a person hears or reads the Word of God as Romans 10:17 says, "Consequently, faith comes from hearing the message, and the message is heard through the Word."

Indeed, as M.J. Zani says, "God's Word is able to pass through any thick wall"—whether the wall be stone, cultural or religious—and it transforms lives.

PRAYER

Praise God that His Word broadcast on radio can go where missionaries and printed words cannot. Praise God for TWR and pray that as people tune in, God's Spirit will speak to them. Pray for "silent nights" so the radio transmission signals travel clearly across the miles.

MEDITATION

My word that goes out from my mouth . . . will not return to me empty, but will accomplish what I desire and achieve the purpose for which I sent it. (Isaiah 55:11)

For the earth will be filled with the knowledge of the glory of the Lord … (Habakkuk 2:14)

REFLECTION

Do I thank God that I can listen to God's Word on the radio any time? What do I do to help others hear His Word?

---

[1] Zani's quote is from *Come Ye Apart*, a devotional booklet of the Nazarene Church.

[2] When a person indicates a desire to receive material, a follow-up coordinator sends it, along with a letter.

[3] Romani is spoken by Gypsies.

13

A "Convert to Killing" Becomes a Convert to Christ

Once known as fierce fighters, the Anga-atiya people of Papua New Guinea danced to celebrate victory in war. Today, they celebrate laying down their weapons and embracing God's Word of peace and hope.
—Wycliffe's prayer publication, the Intercessor

Fausto carefully aimed his gun and pulled the trigger. *Wow! The guy dropped instantly!* he noted. And so, realizing how easy it was to kill, Fausto became a "convert to killing."

Armed groups, motivated by a chilling desire for power, spread terror throughout the city of Bogota, Colombia. Fausto joined one of those guerilla groups. And that day—with his first, but not last, murder—Fausto's little boy innocence was forever shattered. He spent the remainder of his childhood years reveling in violence. Anyone Fausto's gang suspected of collaborating with a rival gang was targeted for execution. Having "earned" the enviable endorsement of police officials, guerilla leaders paid them a service fee to turn a blind eye.

One day someone had the courage to talk with Fausto about God. He opened his Bible and explained that "Jesus, God's Son, loves you. He wants to forgive you and give you a new life." Just as Fausto had readily become an enthusiastic convert to killing, he became an enthusiastic convert to Christ.

One of his first acts as a new person in Christ was to tell his brothers, also members of guerrilla gangs, what happened to him. Over the next few weeks, Caleb and Mario saw the change in their brother's life and listened to him talk about Jesus. They also put their faith in Christ.

Fausto heard about a discipleship seminar run by Open Doors[1] and decided to go. "I used to carry my gun everywhere I went," he told men at the seminar. "I'd use it to take the life of anyone who stood in my way. Now the only weapon I carry is my Bible. I use it to give life to anyone who comes my way and will listen. I want to return and tell my comrades what God has done in my life." Holding up his Bible, he said, "I want to arm my comrades with this weapon."

Open Doors partnered with Fausto to help him fulfill his ambitious project.[2] They enabled him to distribute over a thousand Bibles to his guerrilla comrades. Many read and responded to the Good News of salvation just as Fausto had. But the guerilla leaders had other ideas. "We've gotta stop this guy," they grumbled. "We're losing too many men because of him."

So, in late 1999 Fausto was assassinated. He entered into God's presence, the One he had come to know, the One whose

Word he had shared with so many. At his funeral, as his entire extended family grieved, their despair was replaced by conviction and purpose.

His assassins had met their goal: Kill Fausto! But they were unable to stop his work. After his death, the family asked Open Doors workers, "Please help us. To honor the memory of our brother, husband, and father, we want to distribute Scriptures to his killers and other violent gangs."

Today Fausto's widow, Belinda, and her seven children live in what Open Doors workers would describe as a shack. But Belinda says, "I am thankful for the prayers and support of the body of Christ. My children smile and say they can't believe this mansion actually belongs to us. 'How can we pay the rent, Mommy?' they ask. And I tell them, 'Just as God provided a place in heaven for your daddy, He has provided us with this beautiful house.' "

Bob Nunyea, a Walmajarri pastor in Australia, held up a shield and declared to his people, "Not this shield, but the Word of God is the Christian's most important weapon!" Once Fausto became "a convert to killing," he agreed with Bob Nunyea, and with the apostle Paul who wrote to the Ephesians, "God's Word is an indispensible weapon," (6:17, MSG).

PRAYER

Praise God for Fausto's life! And praise Him that Belinda has a job as a seamstress because Open Doors provided her with a sewing machine. "Someday I want to establish my own clothing business," she says. Pray that she will soon be able to do that. Ask God to protect Open Doors workers as they minister to the suffering church. Pray that guerillas who receive Bibles will read them and come to Christ.

MEDITATION

Even though I was once … a violent man, I was shown mercy because I acted in ignorance and unbelief … (I Timothy 1:13–14)

REFLECTION

Do I have a Fausto-like commitment to see people receive God's Word? Have I learned to give thanks in all circumstances as Fausto's wife has? Am I praying for and giving to some organization committed to providing God's Word for the suffering church?

---

[1]This story is used by permission of Open Doors Australia. Fausto's story first appeared in an "Opendoors Newsbrief."

[2]During its 50-plus years of existence, Open Doors has delivered millions of Bibles and trained thousands of leaders to work with the suffering church around the world.

14

Mega-love Serves Hot Meals

There is no better way to preach to someone than to offer a loaf of bread in one hand and a Bible in the other.
—the Central Church of God, Charlotte, N.C.

"Oh, no!" Pastor Ding Teodoro exclaimed. He and a group of young men were speeding along a country road just outside metropolitan Manila. "I forgot to lock our house and Mona's taken the kids and gone away for the weekend."

"Never mind, Pastor," one of the young men quipped. "You don't have to worry about thieves. All the thieves from your neighborhood are right here with you."

They laughed—well aware that at one time, his words would have had a ring of truth to them. "All these thieves" included him and the other young Filipino men in the van. All had come to a relationship with Jesus Christ in the last two years. Pastor Ding, as his congregation called him, was taking them away for a weekend retreat.

Pastor Ding thought about how this had all begun. *It was the 1999 Christmas season.* Groups of children at their gate calling out "Medi Krismas! Medi Krismas!" Nothing unusual about that; it happened every year. From nearby squatter settlements, children congregated at residential gates all over the neighborhood to deliver greetings in word and song—always grateful for the small gifts of money or food they received.

In another part of the neighborhood, Michael and Treesa Hause,[1] part of Pastor Ding's church leadership team, were likewise prepared with pesos and small packets of food to give to children at their gate. That Christmas, as wave after wave of children arrived, God moved the Hause and Teodoro families to ask themselves, "What more can we do for these hungry children? What can our church do for them?"

"We'll have flyers made in Tagalog . . . They did—church people passed out hundreds of them. "We'll invite children to a Christmas party, serve them a hot lunch, and . . ." They did—about five hundred children showed up and watched a reenactment of the Christmas story. They heard the Gospel, then were served a meal of *lechon* (pork) and spaghetti. "That was the best meal I've had in my whole life!" one child was heard to remark.

After Christmas, the Hauses met with the Teodoros and another missionary couple. A plan was birthed: the church would begin a weekly Bible club for children, and then train them to become leaders in their settlements. On Saturday mornings, children came to the church for a Super Kids Bible Club, followed by a hot lunch—rice with *ulam* topping. Every tenth Saturday, at a "graduation" ceremony, those with perfect attendance received a prize and a bag of food to take home. The number of children enrolled grew from 35 to 50, then to 100, and on up to 300!

At first, the biggest attraction was the hot meal. But as they heard Bible stories about a long ago Jesus who loved children, He became an equal attraction. Many came to know Jesus, not only as the long ago One, but as the eternally present One who still loves children.

The children went home and talked about the club to their parents or parent—in many cases there were no fathers to talk to—and their siblings. Mothers were reported to have said such things as: "My children are different. What's happened to them?" "My boys used to fight. Now they get along." "My children help with chores these days."

A group of street-wise teenage boys from the settlement decided they wanted to check out this new thing their younger siblings were involved in. Some of these teenagers were addicted to drugs. One was a survivor of a recent suicide attempt. Some even had fathers who were thieves or murderers. Others didn't know who their fathers were.

Skeptical, sometimes unruly—but still they came to the Super Kids Bible Club. And because of that free meal, they kept coming. Pastor Ding knew that these teenagers—they were really young men—needed their own group, apart from the children. So he began a Sunday night Bible study with them. Eighteen of them came to know Jesus! It was one of these who had quipped, "Never mind, Pastor, you don't have to worry about thieves . . ."

Last year at the annual Christmas party, Pastor Ding's congregation gave out two thousand bags to the children—a thousand with lunches in them; the other thousand with toys, pens, pencils, erasers—and a snack.

What type of church has done all this evangelism, assembled all those bags, and threw a party for a thousand kids? A megachurch? No, just a church with around 50 adult members. Each with a mega-heart of compassion and enthusiasm, reaching out to the lost and hurting, despite the mega-work involved.

Epilogue
Little girls who first attended the Super Bible Club are now young women. They desire an education that will help them get jobs and earn money so they can help their families and communities. Since these young women have no money for schooling, the Hauses' teenage daughters have come up with a plan to help raise money so they can go to college. At a large open market in metro Manila, Alyssa and Kendra buy uncultured pearl necklaces and earrings for a very reasonable price. They send these to churches and people in the U.S.A. to sell for a small profit.

It is difficult for street children and those who live in squatter areas to go to school; sometimes their families don't even have enough money to buy food. Pastor Ding and his small congregation believe that someday God will provide money to build a dorm and a school for these children and young people—and call people to staff both.

PRAYER

Father, bless Pastor Ding and Mona and the people at New Hope Christian Fellowship in Manila for their labor of love that reaches out to the poor. Pray that the Teodoros and the Hauses, as well as others participating in the ministry with the squatter children, will have strength and continued sensitivity to God's Spirit. Pray for provision of finances so the church can continue holding these clubs.

MEDITATION

Blessed is he who is kind to the needy. (Proverbs 14:21)

But when you give a banquet, invite the poor, the crippled, the lame, the blind, and you will be blessed. (Luke 14:13–14)

REFLECTION

Franklin Graham says, "A hot meal warms the heart as well as nourishes the body, enabling believers to share the Good News of Jesus Christ with those who are starving for His love." What am I doing to help feed the hungry children of the world?

[1]Michael and Treesa Hause are with Wycliffe and serve full-time at Faith Academy in Manila. Faith is an international school, primarily for children of Christian workers throughout Asia. It is administered by a number of different mission organizations. Treesa is the daughter of Ed and Aretta Loving.

15

Though We Can't See God...

Teaching people the Word, showing them love and where to turn in the midst of their pain and confusion, helping them develop and deepen their relationship with Jesus Christ—that is what will make the difference in their difficult circumstances.

—Kay Arthur

A loud cry pierced the air—and from every part of the village people came running. Inside a small hut, they found Ujukuti's old mother frantically trying to unwrap a rope from around her blind son's neck. Despite her frailty, she was holding him up by the leg to keep him from hanging himself.

Ujukuti and his Bassar people in Togo, West Africa, believed blindness was a punishment from the spirits, so blind people were ostracized. Convinced that "for the Blind in Togo there is no hope," Ujukuti knew no other solution to his hopeless state.

As it became obvious that Ujukuti had not succeeded in hanging himself, his mother wailed, "This is the third time he's tried to kill himself."

Many years before, a young American man about the same

age as Ujukuti received devastating news. "You have retinitis pigmentosa, a degenerative disease that kills the cells of the retina and ultimately leads to blindness," his doctor told him. Richard Steele would have to abandon his dream of becoming a medical research scientist. "I wanted to help suffering people," Richard says. "I learned that around a million Americans were suffering from this same disease. And I wouldn't be able to help them."

Unlike Ujukuti, Richard did not try to end his life. Eventually he was even able to say, "God makes no mistakes. My blindness happened for a reason."

Years later, the lives of Ujukuti and Richard—and Abu, another young Bassar man—would intertwine. Both Richard and Abu became a part of the solution to Ujukuti's hopelessness. Ujukuti learned that there is hope for the Blind, even in Togo.

Abu was the first blind student at Centre Bethesaïda pour la Réhabilitation des Aveugles (CBRA), a school for blind students. In primary school, before he became blind, Abu had learned to read and write in French. Abu's passion was music; his skill, composing songs; his goal, to glorify Christ with his gift. After taking Braille courses at the school, with Richard's help, he was able to put his songs on paper, songs that had previously been stored only in his mind.

After hearing of Ujukuti's attempted suicide, Abu convinced Ujukuti to come to CBRA. There, for the first time ever, from Richard and other Christian teachers, he heard the Gospel in his heart language. After asking Jesus Christ to come into his life,

Ujukuti's desire was to go back home—home to the village where he'd tried to kill himself. "I want to tell everyone there what God has done for me."

One Sunday afternoon, Ujukuti and a group from the school walked to his village. Months before, when Ujukuti had left home, villagers had said goodbye to a sad young man—one with no hope. Now his people saw a different young man—one who was joyous and confident.

"We brought guitars and people gathered," Ujukuti says of that visit home. "We sang—some were Abu's songs. My people loved that! It was the first time they had sung Scripture songs in our language. At school, I decided that if these instructors can love me so much, Jesus must love me too. Now I want to tell others about this God who loves us and can change us," he told his people. And they listened to this new Ujukuti. They listened, and responded, when he asked, "Who would like to have what God has given to me?"

That Sunday afternoon, the nucleus of a Christian church was born. Today well over three fourths of the villagers are believers. All because of the witness of a once suicidal young man who — even though he couldn't see those giving love—experienced love he'd never known before. "That's how God's Word in their heart language[1] affects people," Richard says. "They don't have to have outsiders do all the work for them. Our job is to partner with them to put God's Word into their heart language. The Holy Spirit then uses them to evangelize their own people.[2]

PRAYER

Rejoice that even though we can't see God, we can experience His love. Praise Him that His Word gives spiritual sight to those without physical sight. Ask for wisdom and unity for the committee of Bassar men now translating the Old Testament. Thank God for the many years CBRA functioned. Pray for Nyong and several others who follow-up with those who were once at CBRA, continuing to help them with their needs. Praise God for Richard's vision that resulted in CBRA.[3]

MEDITATION

Be sure to fear the Lord and serve him faithfully with all your heart; consider what great things he has done for you. (1 Samuel 12:24)

Are you called to help others? Do it with all the strength and energy that God supplies. Then God will be given glory in everything through Jesus Christ. (1 Peter 4:11, NLT)

REFLECTION

When I help others, do I use my own strength and energy or that which God supplies?

[1]Samuel Nabine was the translator of the Bassar New Testament, dedicated in 1992. Richard worked five weeks, sometimes 15 hours a day, to keyboard the Bassar New Testament into Braille. The 1,826-page, 35-volume New Testament weighs 35-40 pounds and fills a 6-foot-long shelf!

[2]Sitting at his computer, which has a JAWS (Job Acquisition with Speech) card, Richard says, "People wonder why I work here at JAARS Vernacular Media Services (VMS). Not all are able to read and write—even those with sight. Yet they need God's Word as desperately as everyone else. At VMS we're getting the Word to those who can't read, in forms that are not heavy and don't fill 6 feet of shelf space."

[3]It was in 1984 that Richard began developing the concept of a school where sighted Africans could teach Braille to the Blind. "I wanted to help them not only read but also attain skills such as animal husbandry and farm work, so they could help themselves," Richard says. After many successful years, the school closed due to fewer cases of blindness. The World Health Organization (WHO) began spraying rivers and streams, killing the filarial eggs, which had led to large numbers of people losing their eyesight. A WHO Internet report on river blindness reads: "Onchocerciasis is an eye and skin disease caused by a worm (filarial) . . . It is the world's second leading infectious cause of blindness."

16

"Why Us, Lord?"

When the Word came to our people, literacy started. People learned to read, they read it, they became Christians.

—Grace Adjekum, Ghana, GILLBT

The bitterly cold February night in Kitchener, Ontario, didn't stop Bob and Jean Schmitt from going to an evening service at their church. Horst and Eugenie Schulz,[1] representatives of Lutheran Bible Translators (LBT) Canada, were speaking at the Schmitts' church, Holy Cross Lutheran.

The Schmitts felt content living in Canada. Bob, a schoolteacher, enjoyed his work. To supplement their income, Jean looked after their three children and baby-sat for others in their home. Sunday School, choir and other church activities kept them more than busy. "We were so happy working right at home in God's Kingdom," Bob says. "That night we heard of LBT's need for literacy workers, And we were hooked." They began to move in obedience toward serving with LBT as literacy workers.[2] "God steered us by opening some doors and closing others."

"Why us, Lord?" both Bob and Jean asked.

And God's Spirit spoke to them from His Word: "The harvest is plentiful but the workers are few" (Matthew 9:37).

In the following months and years, they asked themselves that same question—"Why us, Lord?"—again and again, as well as many other questions. And God always answered with His Word.

When in training, sick and overwhelmed by the difficulty of studies—"How can we cope, Lord?"

The answer came: "I will strengthen you and help you; I will uphold you with my righteous right hand" (Isaiah 41:10).

When leaving to go overseas, homesick for friends, family and familiar surroundings—"When will we see our family and our country again, Lord?"

"And everyone who has left . . . brothers or sisters or father or mother . . . for my sake will receive a hundred times as much and will inherit eternal life" (Matthew 19:29).

Adjusting to a hot, dusty place in West Africa, erratic water flow, unreliable electrical power supply, often no food in stores—"What are we doing here anyway? When will we get to the job you sent us to do, Lord?"

"Your times are in my hands" (see Psalm 31:15).

Their first days in the village—camping out on the concrete floor of their new house with no furniture; no electricity (not even an unreliable source as previously); water supplied only by rain; seeing no familiar faces; hearing a language they did not understand;

immersed in customs so very different from their own—"How can we love these people? Help us, Lord!"

"I have poured out my love into your hearts by the Holy Spirit" (see Romans 5:5).

Several months later, aware of the bondage in which Satan held the Limba people and the fear he covered them with—"How can we reach these people with the saving Gospel of Jesus Christ? What can we do?"

"I will instruct you and teach you in the way you should go …" (Psalm 32:8).

"After lots of prayer for direction, we ran a test class using the Limba literacy materials," Jean says. "That proved extremely successful. People learned to read and write Limba in seven months and began to read the Limba New Testament[3] out loud in church." Then after more prayer, they began another class. "We invited only the 'big' men. We figured if these older men could learn to read and write their language, they could read the New Testament for themselves."

The village chief and elders eagerly accepted the special invitation. Classes began with enthusiasm. But never mind the difficulty these older men had deciphering those tiny marks on paper—a number of them soon realized that even seeing those marks clearly was more difficult than they had imagined. The chief quickly solved his problem: *I'll send Abdulai in my place*, he decided.

Abdulai's culture taught him to respect and obey his elders, especially his parents. So, though now past twenty-one, he obeyed his father. But his obedience didn't cause him to be a happy-camper. "This stuff is for babies and old men," he grumbled.

"Maybe we ought to ask him to not come back," Bob suggested. "He really disrupts the whole class." But their problem student was a bright young man. While they put Bob's maybe-suggestion on hold, Abdulai, in spite of himself, quickly became the star student of the class once those funny marks on paper started to make sense to him.

"Our beginning frustrations had often made us wonder if it was worth it all," Jean reports. "But now Abdulai and others who had never held a pencil or a book were reading and writing in their own language. And the most exciting thing—they could now read their own New Testaments!"

Weeks passed with the Schmitts basking in the joy of how things were progressing. Then Abdulai began coming each afternoon asking for aspirin. Day after day he came with the same complaint: "My head aches!"

What's wrong? the Schmitts wondered. *Maybe we should take him to a doctor . . .* But one day, instead of talking about a headache, Abdulai announced, "I want to become a Christian. And I want to be baptized."

Where, they wondered, *did he learn about the Lord? He doesn't go to church.*

"Abdulai, who told you about Jesus?"

"No one."

"But how do you know about Him?" Bob persisted.

Abdulai held out a dog-eared Limba New Testament. "After taking my father's place and learning to read, I've been reading this Book."

Now Bob and Jean understood. Eyes unaccustomed to focusing on print for hours each day—no wonder his head ached. Bob had another question before agreeing to Abdulai's request. "Why do you want to be baptized?"

"Because I've read this Book and I now see that following Jesus is the right way," he answered with confidence.

At his baptism, Abdulai testified, "I believed because for the first time I understood what God was saying to me." After that, he burned his charms, giving a powerful proclamation to the community: "I no longer live in fear. I'm free from Satan's bondage! He can't harm me now, because Jesus is stronger than him!"

"Why us, Lord?" the Schmitts had asked again and again.

The answer couldn't have been clearer: "That Abdulai and many of his people might read my Word in their heart language and come to know me."

They no longer ask, "Why us, Lord?" Rather with joy, they say, "Why not us, Lord!"

PRAYER

The Schmitts ask that we "Praise God for dedicated national workers around the world who passionately want their people to have His Word in their heart languages!" Pray for the Schmitts as they now work with Lutheran Bible Translators in Canada.[4] Praise God that despite war, work among the Limba has continued. Pray that Abdulai and other Limba Christians will remain firm in their faith.

MEDITATION

He is to write . . . on a scroll a copy of this law . . . It is to be with him, and he is to read it all the days of his life so that he may learn to revere the Lord his God and follow carefully all the words of this law and these decrees . . . (Deuteronomy 17:18–19)

Whether you turn to the right or to the left, your ears will hear a voice behind you, saying, "This is the way; walk in it." (Isaiah 30:21)

REFLECTION

Most of have asked, "Why me, Lord?" At such times, do I press on to follow God's call on my life, as the Schmitts have?

---

[1]For many years, as dual members with both LBT Canada and Wycliffe, the Schulzes served in Papua New Guinea. There, with their technical skills, they supported Bible translators, some who were also serving jointly with LBT and Wycliffe. See Appendix B for more on Lutheran Bible Translators.

[2]Literacy workers train literacy supervisors, who in turn, train others to teach reading classes; help people develop primers (books that introduce the alphabet and teach people to read); train people to write reading material; and in all ways, encourage literacy.

[3]The translation of the Limba New Testament was facilitated by John and Joanne Iler of LBT and published by The Korean Bible Society. "We were blessed to arrive on time for the New Testament dedication in 1983," Bob says.

[4]Today Bob serves as LBT Canada's Executive Director, and Jean continues to support the ministry and still baby-sits in their home in Kitchener.

17

"He's a Changed Man!"

I used to beat my wife. But now I've read in God's Book that a husband and wife are not "another person, another person." So if I beat my wife, that's the same as beating my own body.

—Puansehmo, an Awa man in Papua New Guinea

"I thank God for Esaie," said Ester, a Gban woman of Cote d'Ivoire,[1] West Africa.

What were these women at the Gban conference hearing? Ester thanking God for her husband? How could a wife thank God for an abusive husband?

Usually a quiet and unassuming lady, Ester stood and, in her Gban language, spoke enthusiastically at a church conference for women. Her face glowed as she told her friends why she was thankful for her husband.

"Esaie used to come home from the fields, throw his machete down, then swallow some drink and begin chewing tobacco. He wouldn't even eat the food I cooked for him. He was quarrelsome, and sometimes he beat me."

She lowered her voice. "My family urged me to leave him. But Esaie and I have four children. So I said no. How could I leave the father of my children?"

Ester smiled as she continued her story. "A close friend of Esaie's decided to 'put his heart with Jesus' and one day he invited Esaie to church. At first my husband scoffed at the idea. 'Hmmf! Me go to church?' But finally he went. And there he found something good—books written in our Gban language!

"Esaie never went to school and he knows only a little French. But when he found those books, he taught himself to read from them. While I cooked our food, Esaie would sit and read. I'd see him tracing under the words with his finger as he read out loud. Now my husband is a changed man. When he gets home from work, he sits quietly and reads."

Ester stopped and laughed. "Every once in awhile, when he reads something that's really good, he interrupts himself with a *'Die yo!'* or sometimes, when something he reads surprises him, I hear him exclaim *'Hiin!'*

"He's read those books—the Gospel of Mark and Acts—so often that now he knows all of Mark and most of Acts by heart."

Ah, no wonder Ester thanks God for her husband. He has heeded God's command: "Husbands, love your wives as Christ loved the church and gave himself for it" (Ephesians 5:21).

Not only does he no longer beat his wife, he now eats the food she cooks for him! And he hungers and thirsts for God's Word. He is devouring words written in the language that speaks to his heart!

PRAYER

The Gban New Testament was dedicated in late 1999. Praise God that the Word of God has power to change wife beaters into God lovers. Pray for Pastor Kouassi Danon Alfred and Mr. Taki Oya Thomas, the main translators who assisted Olive Howard of Worldwide Evangelical Crusade (WEC), coordinator of the Gban translation project.

MEDITATION

You don't hang out at Sin Saloon . . . Instead you thrill to God's Word, you chew on Scripture day and night. (Psalm 1:1–2, MSG)

Study this book of the Law continually. Meditate on it day and night so you may be sure to obey all that is written in it. Only then will you succeed. (Joshua 1:8, NLT)

REFLECTION

Has God's Word changed my life? If so, in what ways? Do I often let days go by without reading His Word?

---

[1] Cote d'Ivoire is the French name for Ivory Coast

18

"I'll Never Go Back!"

*Throughout the centuries, people from many lands have opened this book
[the Bible] and have read from it in their own languages. Here they have
learned about God's love and justice . . .*
— **"User's Guide to Beneficial Bible Study," CEV**

"Daddy, come to church with me and I'll get a prize." Four-year-old Spencer's request caused negative feelings to surface in John Perkins. He loved his son but . . .

"My background had prejudiced me against the church, specifically the black church, the only one I knew anything about. My family had rejected the church, looking on it as a tool to make a person weak and dependent—just one more kind of exploitation of black people.

"I couldn't even imagine something called a 'white Christian.' I found it impossible to consider that the white church, the private club of the oppressors, had anything to do with reality and justice."

In 1946 when John was 16 years old, the ultimate injustice

occurred. The war had ended and his brother Clyde had returned home. One Saturday evening, an angry town marshal shot and killed Clyde in a racial incident. "They closed his coffin and it was all over. We all knew there would be no official inquiry."

The next year John took a train to California. "Mississippi was behind me. *Forever*, I told myself." But John did return to Mississippi for a visit—and met Vera Mae. Two years later they married.

The son of a sharecropper, John grew up in the midst of poverty and oppression, just a few notches above slavery. "After a few years in California, I had achieved my goal: to make it in life. I worked with a good company and was really getting somewhere. Despite that, both Vera Mae and I were searching. She was going to church haphazardly. I'd go with her and I wondered a lot."

That wondering led John into short involvements with a couple of cults. "Then in 1957, in a quiet way, God began to show me the unimaginable," he says. "Vera Mae sent Spencer to a children's Bible class in a little church down the street. He'd come home real happy. In those days we just sat down and ate. But Spencer wanted to pray and say Bible verses before meals."

And Spencer kept after his father to "Come to church with me, Daddy!"

"Something was happening to Spencer—something I knew nothing about. I'd not seen Christianity at work like that in anyone's life. At work in a beautiful way. Because I loved my son, I finally went with him. Besides, I wanted to find out what they taught to make Spencer such a radiant little boy. I found they were simply teaching the Bible."

For years, a friend from work had been inviting John to church. "Vera Mae and the kids had gone to his church. Calvin finally persuaded me to go. I met zealous Christians; folks you could feel loved you. These black men told me they had found 'meaning in life through Christ.' Their words had a ring to them."

John joined a church Bible class on the apostle Paul. "I was 27 years old, yet this was my first encounter with the Bible as a real book. I had considered it as full of old wives' tales. Why would any intelligent person bother to read the Bible?"

But "read the Bible" John did. "Every day I studied my Bible. And every week I joined in class discussions and asked questions."

John saw Paul as someone like himself: super-motivated. "I was motivated for my economic betterment. Paul's motivation was unselfish. His was a religious motivation." All summer two questions hounded John: *How could religion mean so much to anyone?* and *What made Paul tick?*

"I had to find the answers," he says. He bought a commentary on Acts, and as summer moved into fall—more study, more questions, more discussions. "This guy Paul was getting to me. He endured so much just for religion. I still hadn't seen anything in religion that would cause someone to give up his life and endure what Paul suffered. To me, religion was not something to suffer for. It was something to suffer with."

One night John read: "I am crucified with Christ: nevertheless

I live; yet not I, but Christ liveth in me: and the life which I now live in the flesh I live by the faith of the Son of God, who loved me, and gave himself for me" (Galatians 2:20, KJV).

"For the first time, the Holy Spirit spoke to me through the Bible. You know," John says, "I'd never before heard that being a Christian was Christ living in me and I living out my life in Him. I didn't have that kind of life. All I had was an ulcer—and I wasn't yet 30. The life Paul talked about came from yielding to Christ. Just the opposite of my self-pushing. Despite my drive, I didn't have Paul's contentment."

The next Sunday, the pastor preached on Romans 6:23: "For the wages of sin is death; but the gift of God is eternal life through Jesus Christ our Lord" (KJV). "That verse hit me hard right in my interest and motivation. I knew about wages. Wages were what I was paid in Mississippi when I was old enough to work hard, but still young enough that a white employer could excuse himself from paying his black laborer a decent wage. I knew about 'the wages of sin.' At my job, union organizers talked about 'stopping exploitation.' My boyhood experiences taught me what exploitation meant: exploitation was sin! But *my* sin? Back and forth from life to Scripture my mind went."

That morning John saw that his sin was against a holy God who loved him. "I surrendered to Him and sensed the beginning of a new life filling the emptiness within—even on payday. I didn't have solutions to my struggles, but I had an inward peace for the first time in my life."

John moved into this new life like he did everything else—as hard as he could. "Right away I began talking to neighbors about Jesus. Fellow church members who had thought I was a Christian saw real changes in me. And my salvation caused my whole family to dedicate themselves to the Lord Jesus."

Vera Mae had come to know Christ as a young girl through Child Evangelism Fellowship (CEF). Now she and John began taking weekly CEF teacher-training workshops and teaching a class to their neighborhood children. "One thing about us—when we get involved, it's all or nothing," John says.

"In the workshops I met, not just white church members, but white Christians. It's hard to describe how different that was for me. First, God had shown me black people changed by the Gospel. Now He showed me that the Gospel had power to change even whites."

John joined with a group ministering in youth detention camps. "Most of those teens were blacks with accents like guys I grew up with. Some were sons of men who had fled the deep South as I had." A conviction began to grow in John that God wanted him back in Mississippi. "I felt God wanted me to identify with my people there. To help break the cycle of despair—not by encouraging them to leave, but by showing them new life right where they were."

One Sunday as he preached from Romans 10, God confirmed to John's spirit: "My desire is that you return. Your people have a zeal for God, but it is not enlightened."

"I remembered the emotionalism I'd seen. Most black preachers pastored four or five churches at once and had little opportunity for real Bible training. After that morning, I was never again satisfied in California."

The man who had vowed, "I'll never go back!" left his secure job and home in California, and in 1960 returned to Mendenhall, Mississippi, where he had lived as a child.

God for a black man? John had asked himself. Now he answers, "Yes! God for a black man. This black man. Me!" And he knew that God was for his people.[1]

Epilogue

Today Dr. Perkins says, "I'm 76 now and doors are open all across the country for me to teach my unique brand of the Gospel—combining evangelism, reconciliation and justice to rebuild poor communities." Many centuries ago, another man who had suffered also practiced the unique brand of the Gospel that Dr. Perkins practices today. That man said,

> *I put on righteousness, and it clothed me;*
> *My justice was like a robe and a turban.*
> *I was eyes to the blind,*
> *And I was feet to the lame.*
> *I was a father to the poor,*
> *And I searched out the case that I did not know.*
> *I broke the fangs of the wicked,*
> *And plucked the victim from his teeth.*

(Job 29:14–17, NKJV)

PRAYER

Spencer went to be with his Lord in 1998. Praise God for his life. Pray that God will continue to give strength to Dr. John. Pray for the continued outreach of the multiple ministries of the John M. Perkins Foundation (JMPF) for Reconciliation and Development. Pray about taking a work / teaching trip to the campus.[2]

MEDITATION

Your people will rebuild the ancient ruins and will raise up the age-old foundations; you will be called Repairer of Broken Walls, Restorer of Streets with Dwellings … (Isaiah 58:12)

Brethren, my heart's desire and prayer to God for [my people] is, that they might be saved. They have a zeal for God, but not according to knowledge. (Romans 10:1–2, KJV)

REFLECTION

Like Dr. John, have I realized that my sin is against a holy God? Do I have a concern for reconciliation with and justice for people discriminated against?

[1] Despite having only a third grade education, Dr. Perkins is a humble, joyful man who has received eight honorary doctorates and authored eight books. This story was compiled from one of those books: *Let Justice Roll Down*, Regal Books, 1976. Dr. Perkins has revised and updated this book and Regal will have it on the market in December 2006.

[2] Dr. Perkins and his wife Vera May invite churches to bring workgroups to help with the continued development of the John M. Perkins Foundation for Reconciliation and Development (JMPF) campus in Jackson, Mississippi. While there, they receive training in mission outreach. (Appendix C describes the ministries of JMPF.)

19
They Have Heard and Seen God's Word

I'd heard about the gospel but never really understood. Now I've seen it with my own eyes, and I believe.

—a Kekchi farmer, Guatemala

His new job filled his mind, pushing out any thought for the Kekchi workers on his *finca* (plantation). *The supervisors will handle everything*, he concluded.

And so Carlos Pacay, with hardly a backward look, left his large coffee-growing *finca* in the rugged Guatemalan mountains to take up a job with the Embassy in Argentina.

"Thirty years ago, life was hard for the Kekchi," Carlos says. "The walls of their houses were made of sticks. Most of their salary—only five or ten cents a day—went to buy *chicha* (sugar cane liquor). They were a fearful people and they distrusted us landowners. They even distrusted each other. We couldn't understand what they were afraid of." According to Carlos, the Kekchi people were "the same today as they were when their Mayan ancestors ruled the land centuries ago."

Corn and beans and coffee trees, planted in some of the richest soil in Guatemala, flourish in the cool, moist climate where the Kekchi live. Even on the mountainsides almost anything put in the ground grows. The only thing that didn't grow well, until recently, was faith in Jesus Christ.

Christianity came to the Kekchi people in the 16th century on the heels of the Spanish conquistadores. A mixture of Christian beliefs and their traditional rituals and gods created a Kekchi society that resisted belief in the true God.

Early in the 1900s, missionaries began sowing the seed of God's Word. Fifty years later, Wycliffe translators Fran Eachus and Ruth Carlson were invited by William Sedat, a German missionary with the Church of the Nazarene mission, to work among the Kekchi. Fran and Ruth continued working with the Kekchis for 49 years.

The fear of the Kekchi that had baffled Carlos? "Parents avoided speaking their newborn baby's name aloud, lest the mountain god come and steal its soul," says Fran, who still works with the Kekchi. "Before digging in their gardens, people made a sacrifice to appease the spirits."

As the Bible was translated, seeds began to sprout in the hard soil of Kekchi hearts. One by one, people trusted Christ. Then in 1981, the *JESUS* film,[1] translated into Kekchi, softened the soil and was used by God to reap a ripening harvest.

Jose and Maria Yat became part of that harvest. Maria's sister, after going to a traditional healer, had put a curse on the family. Only five of the Yat's ten children were still alive. And all of them were sickly. *Maybe the shaman can help us*, they decided.

"Yes," the shaman agreed, "I can remove the curse. But first, you must pay 200 *quetzales*."

Jose cleared 100 *quetzales* (approximately $40) from his coffee trees that year, and Maria made about four *quetzales* a day selling her tortillas in the market. How could they possibly pay 200 *quetzales*?

"Let's go to the church down the road. Maybe the people there will help us," Maria suggested. Jose had no interest in church, but he had noticed that the people at that church didn't argue, and they treated each other kindly, unlike the people in his neighborhood. So he went with an attitude of *What do we have to lose?*

"You must see the *JESUS* film," excited people at the church told them.

Pastor Domingo Tzub of the Nazarene church in the nearby town was also excited about the *JESUS* film. "We're showing it everywhere—in homes, on *fincas*, in schools, even in markets where people sell vegetables. About three thousand have come out to see it and about two-thirds of them have trusted Jesus after seeing the film," he reported. Thirteen churches, made up of those new believers, were established.

Jose invited his neighbors to "come see the film that Pastor Domingo will show right here at my house." And they came— squeezing in between his house and the coffee trees. With eyes riveted on the screen, people watched in awe. "They're speaking our language!" was repeated throughout the audience. "Many of the men cried when watching the Crucifixion scene. They lowered their sombreros so nobody would see their tears," Pastor Domingo reported.

That week as Jose chopped firewood in the mountains, he

revisited the vivid scenes and pondered the words from Luke's Gospel. When he and his sons were spreading coffee beans to dry, he said, "My sons, let me tell you what I've seen and heard . . ." His sons listened.

And they also listened as Pastor Domingo came to teach them. "I taught them about the true God who created their mountains and about His Son who died for them."

Eventually Jose and his whole family believed. They began attending the church down the road—the church where people had helped them and not asked for pay.

Today Maria, with a large basket of freshly-made tortillas balanced on her head, sings as she goes to market. She's at peace with her husband, with her neighbors—and with God.

When Carlos returned from Argentina, his workers threw a welcome home fiesta for him. *What has changed these people?* he wondered. They were no longer reserved. One Kekchi stepped up to a microphone and expressed himself fluently. Almost everybody played a new instrument not seen among them before.

Carlos soon discovered what had made the difference: They had seen the *JESUS* film, and now they were following Jesus. "These new Christians are more cooperative," he noted, "and they work more enthusiastically." His *finca* produced more, thus enabling him to pay higher wages. "Without a doubt, religion has bettered the lot of the Kekchi more than anything else. But," he added, "were it not for the cardamom they grow, they would still be living in poverty."

But Pastor Domingo has a different view of things: "People

can make good money, but if God's peace is not in their homes, it's worthless. Today these people respect, love and honor each other. The Gospel teaches good stewardship. The Kekchis used to spend most of their money on *chicha*. Not anymore! When they sell their crops, they fix up their homes. Today I see beds, chairs and tables in their houses.

"Their weeklong religious festivals now have a different focus. No longer is the goal to drink, worship patron saints, or stage elaborate dances to appease evil spirits. Their goal is to celebrate their new faith. They gather in plazas and sing praises to God. Mornings often begin with classes on public health, afternoons are usually for teaching believers, and evenings for preaching the Gospel. This new focus has produced healthier and happier Kekchis."

Joyful believers have spread God's message wherever they go. Churches dot the valleys. The Gospel has been planted as solidly among the Kekchi as the mountains are planted in the earth—all this because of God's Word translated into their language, and then presented visually. Indeed, they have both heard and seen the Gospel in their heart language.[2]

PRAYER

Praise God for the cooperation among mission organizations, which has resulted in thousands of Kekchi people becoming believers.[3] Pray that these believers will stand steadfast in their faith. Praise God for Campus Crusade's New Life Training Centers (NLTC) where believers are trained to win others to Christ, help new believers grow, then "reseed" themselves by leading others to Christ.[4]

MEDITATION

They said to the woman, "We no longer believe just because of what you said; now we have heard [and seen] for ourselves, and we know that this man really is the Savior of the world." (John 4:42)

This same Good News that came to you is going out all over the world. It is changing lives everywhere, just as it changed yours that very first day you heard and understood the truth about God's great kindness to sinners. (Colossians 1:6, NLT)

REFLECTION

Have you considered purchasing a *JESUS* CD or video and inviting your neighbors in to see it?

---

[1]The *JESUS* film has been translated into over nine hundred languages and distributed in countries around the world by The JESUS Film Project, a ministry of Campus Crusade for Christ International. See Appendix B for more on The JESUS Film Project and The Luke Partnership.

[2]This story was compiled from two stories by Bill Sundstrom from Campus Crusade's *Worldwide Challenge* magazine.

[3]Wycliffe facilitated the translation of the Kekchi Bible. The Nazarene, Southern Baptist and many other denominational missions and churches have shown the *JESUS* film, and all consider it one of the most important tools for proclaiming the Gospel.

[4]Where there is no established church, NLTC graduates begin Bible studies in homes. These Bible studies often grow into a church sponsored by a denomination.

20

"I Can't, Lord!"

I can do all things through Christ who strengthens me.
—**the apostle Paul, Philippians 4:13 (NKJV)**

"I can't, Lord! Somebody else will have to," Nancy Lightfoot told God. Serving with the United Methodist Church (UMC)[1], Nancy had been in Liberia, West Africa, for almost ten years.

In the 1960s, UMC Bishop Nagbe of Liberia requested a linguist to analyze and propose an alphabet for the Klao language. A beginning grammar was written, a primer constructed, and some people were being taught to read.

Assigned to coordinate adult literacy and literature production with the Klao, Nancy arrived on the scene in 1972. "A Klao man and I traveled to Ghana to get help from Wycliffe. For three months each day, that faithful Klao man whistled so I could hear his language tone and learn how the system worked. Back in Monrovia, I wrote a new primer and taught an adult reading class."

For seven years Nancy collected stories, learned more grammar, wrote more books and taught adult reading classes. Part of that time, Sharon Poellot of Lutheran Bible Translators (LBT) worked with her. Despite their efforts, frustrating years slipped by with little response from the Klao people. "Why don't they want to learn to read?" Nancy and her co-workers lamented. They brainstormed and came up with the simple answer: "They don't have the one Book they really want to read—the Bible in Klao."

"On Sundays, second and third generation missionized Klao attended church and heard the Bible read in English, often not even a modern version," Nancy says.

The United Bible Society (UBS) encouraged Nancy to translate the Bible into Klao. "I can't!" Nancy insisted. "Somebody else will have to."

"We believe you can do it," UBS personnel affirmed. Still, month after month Nancy prayed, "Lord, speak to someone to translate your Word for these people." And God did speak to someone . . .

"After three years of arguing with God, I finally realized 'someone' was me," Nancy says. "I told God, 'Okay, I'll do it. But I will really need help.' "

I will help you, my child, Nancy felt God whisper to her spirit.

He began by providing a team of men to work on the translation with Nancy. In 1984 UBS held a translator selection workshop. Humphrey Kumeh, a government worker, was invited. "No, I can't quit my secure job," he told Nancy.

"Come to the workshop anyway," Nancy urged. He came and that week, he and another man, Nynati Sayon, were invited to become translators for their people by the UBS workshop leader.

Nancy states, "I had expected the translation to impact Klao people right from the beginning. But I was surprised at the impact it had on me early on. A back-translation of a first draft of John 1:1-2, 14 reads:

> Before the world was made, the person who is called The Word was living. He and God were together. God was not different. From the beginning he and God were together. Then the person called The Word got in human form, and he lived among us…

"When I read that, it hit me as never before that this 'person' who was with God, and was God, left Heaven's glory and came to earth to live with sinful people. What a Savior—alive and working today!"

Despite all the civil unrest in Liberia, God worked miracles to bring the Klao New Testament to completion. "I often wonder if other Bible translations required as many miracles," Nancy says. Those miracles involved everything from book-eating termites to men-killing rebels. "Termites ate into a book we needed when translating Matthew. But they destroyed only the chapters we had already translated.

"And the rebels—well, while Humphrey and I were in Jerusalem studying Hebrew, Nynati stayed in Liberia to finish spelling corrections in the translation. War broke out in Monrovia and rebels were systematically killing all men who tried to pass through a certain checkpoint. Fleeing the violence, Nynati presented his literacy certificate at that checkpoint. The rebels carefully studied it, then allowed him through!"

In 1993, after a time in the U.S. and unable to return to Liberia because of the war, Nancy went to Cote d'Ivoire. "As rebels in Liberia burned villages, men who had worked on the translation arrived at a refuge camp in Cote d'Ivoire. One by one, all but one of them showed up—even the reviewers.[2] Only Nynati, our best proofreader, was missing. We feared he was dead. But seven years later, he appeared just in time to check the final draft!"

Nancy relates other miracles. "Printed copies of the Gospel of John were looted. We reprinted. Those too were looted. This time, copies appeared in markets all over Monrovia. Looted material sells cheaply; therefore lots of people bought copies. Looters proved to be our best distributors of John's Gospel."

Later, floppy disks with a ready-to-be-printed copy of the New Testament on them were lost, then found; lost, found again—five different times. The last time, someone traveling to the U.S. took the final, proofread from cover-to-cover copy in his suitcase. The airline lost the suitcase. "We immediately asked people to pray. After two weeks, a group of children began praying. The next morning the airline phoned. The lost suitcase had been found!"

Each time something new "opens her mouth" (amazes her), Nancy is reminded of who is in control. "It would take a whole book to tell of all the 'mouth opening' things that have gone into this translation."

Epilogue

Nancy Lightfoot, faithful servant of Jesus Christ, entered heaven on January 12, 2001. A year after the dedication of the Klao New Testament, she was the victim of an auto accident in Liberia. "A Celebration of Her Life and Work" service was held in Michigan, her home state. An excerpt from a letter written by her mother reads: "The story of Nancy's leadership in the completion of the Klao New Testament is both amazing and immensely satisfying. However, her legacy is also the example she provided and the training of her team to carry on. The team of Old Testament translators remains intact."

PRAYER

Praise God that Nancy was obedient to God's calling. Praise Him for the cooperation of the UBS and Wycliffe with GBGM. Pray that the Word in Klao will speak clearly to pastors and that they will preach from it. Pray for Humphrey, Nynati and others now translating the Old Testament.

MEDITATION

He holds victory in store for the upright, he is a shield to those whose walk is blameless, for he guards the course of the just and protects the way of his faithful ones. (Proverbs 2:7–8)

REFLECTION

Have I considered the fact that no circumstance—not even war—can stop God's agenda? Am I taking time to read the Word regularly so God can use it to speak to me, as He spoke to Pastor Philip and Nancy?

---

[1]The mission arm of UMC is known as the General Board of Global Ministries (GBGM).

[2]Reviewers read a translation and give advice on the naturalness of the language. Both laypeople and church leaders serve as reviewers.

21

Looking for a Better Life

God in heaven is just so good. So the people who live in this world, if God's heart is happy with them, then their fear is all gone now.
—Luke 2:14 (back-translation from a language with no specific word for "peace")

Life in Peru was hard and uncertain for Luis and Natalia Vasquez. Luis struggled to make a living for his family. Finally they moved to Tampa, Florida—looking for "a better life."

Meanwhile, Bruce and Alba Sewell, working in Mexico with UFM (now CrossWorld), faced a difficult decision: *Will we send our children to the U.S. for schooling?* The whole family prayed and agonized over this decision.

"Pray and decide if you feel good about going to the States for high school without Mom and Dad," Bruce told their children. A unanimous "We don't feel good about it" confirmed what the parents, as well as relatives in the States, had been feeling all along. The Sewells had just wanted to make sure they weren't forsaking their call to serve God in Mexico.

So it was that in 1995 Bruce and Alba and their four children moved to Florida. CrossWorld has no outreach in the States, therefore mission leaders recommended that the Sewells align themselves with the American Missionary Fellowship (AMF).[1] With their mission's blessing, Bruce and Alba began an outreach to Hispanics in the Greater Tampa Bay area under AMF. Part of that outreach included a Spanish Bible study in a Cuban friend's home.

"One evening I felt we should study a passage with a salvation theme," Bruce says. "The old familiar John 3 was my choice."

Natalia, still looking for "a better life," came to that Bible study. There she heard from God's Word that He loved her—Natalia. He loved her so much that he gave His beloved Son to die for her sins. "That night the Lord nudged me to give an invitation for people to respond to Jesus' offer," Bruce says. And that night Natalia abandoned her search for a better life and entered into the best life: eternal life that God promises to "whoever believes in Him"—Jesus Christ!

Today Natalia faithfully attends those Bible studies and also the Spanish services that Bruce leads in his home church, Christ Community Church. With a glowing face, she testifies, "Once my life was ruled by fear of death. Now God's peace is in my heart. I'm not afraid to die. I know when I die I'll go right to heaven."

And Luis?

"My husband noticed good changes in me," Natalia says. "And he spends more time with our three children. Sometimes he even comes to church with me. When we talk, he brings up God's name in our conversations."

Taking advantage of discounts Luis gets through the travel agency in which he is a partner, the Vasquezes travel to Lima several times a year. Natalia talks to her family about her new faith in Christ. Recently she showed the *JESUS* video in Spanish, then left a copy with her family to show to others.

On these trips to Peru, Luis and Natalia often visit their former home in Iquitos, located in the heart of the Amazon River rainforest. There they give out medicine and clothes to the sick and needy. "We do this in the name of Jesus," Natalia says. She recognizes that she, like these people, was "sick," in need of healing from sin. Her "clothes" were tattered and dirty. Jesus healed her and clothed her with a new robe—His own righteousness. He was indeed the Omega of her search for a better life.

After a fruitful 15-year church planting and Bible Institute ministry in Mexico, Bruce had wondered, *Will the Lord ever use us again to reach people for Christ outside the U.S.?*

"Through discipleship of Natalia and others, the Lord is using our family to bring the Gospel to several Hispanic countries," Bruce now testifies. "Yes, it's our whole family. Our four kids go with me to services at the Pan de Vida Christian Mission in nearby Plant City. Our two older boys and I have formed a soccer team for the migrant boys. Each summer all four help at Vacation Bible Schools. Under AMF, God has given us a part in world evangelism—reaching even to the Peruvian Amazon River jungle."

PRAYER
Praise God that Natalia is studying the Bible on her own. Pray for Luis and Natalia and their children. Praise God that the Sewell children have a part in their parents' ministry. Pray they will continue to follow the Lord strongly. Pray for the Sewells and their ministry to Hispanics in Florida.

MEDITATION
Since the children have flesh and blood, he too shared in their humanity so that by his death he might destroy him who holds the power of death—that is, the devil— and free those who all their lives were held in slavery by their fear of death. (Hebrews 2:14–15)

"I am the Alpha and the Omega," says the Lord God, "who is, and who was, and who is to come, the Almighty." (Revelation 1:8)

REFLECTION
Have I considered that the Lord can use me in my homeland to bring Jesus to people from other countries?

---

[1]In 36 U.S. states, around 170 missionary families serve with AMF full-time or part-time in rural, urban, and suburban areas.

22

A Visual Expression
of the Word of God

As a printer, I could make lots of money printing for secular companies. But when I am tempted to do this, I look into the eyes of those who long for the Word, and then I run back to print more Bibles.
—An underground Bible printer in China

Louise Bass, an artist, lives in Traverse City, Michigan, a tourist resort city in the U.S. Naibei, a farmer, lives on the slopes of Mt. Elgon in Kenya, East Africa.

When Louise was a child, her parents told her Bible stories. They also read the Bible and other books to her. In the Mt. Elgon culture, grandmothers are the storytellers, so it would have been Naibei's grandmother who told him stories. But neither she nor Naibei's parents read the Bible or other books to him, for there was no Bible—no books of any kind—in their language. Naibei's Sabaot language was an oral language; it had never been written.

A few years ago, Bible Translation and Literacy (BTL) in Kenya needed an artist to illustrate reading books and Scripture portions for new literates. For many years Louise had drunk deeply from God's Word, so her ears were attuned to the Holy Spirit's prompting regarding BTL's need. She went to Kenya and volunteered her expertise.[1]

For many years Naibei too had drunk deeply—from a bottle. One day a Scripture book published by BTL fell into his hands. In awe, he whispered, "My Sabaot language has been written!" Though he did not read the book, a picture captured his attention. He stared at it: a shepherd holding a lamb. The caption read: "Jesus is the Good Shepherd." That picture and those words imprinted themselves in his mind and on his heart.

In 1997 Naibei's wife, Beatrice, attended the dedication of the Sabaot New Testament. Though she could not read, she bought two copies of the New Testament. Carefully, she placed them on a shelf in their house. And there they lay, collecting dust.

One night Naibei stumbled home in a drunken stupor and collapsed onto his bed. As he slept, he saw a wounded sheep enter the house. He jumped up and ran outside. A wild beast has attacked my flock, he cried out. At this point Naibei's dream turned into a nightmare. "I'll kill it!" he yelled. He fought the ferocious creature but soon realized he wasn't able to kill it. He ran to his father's house and returned with a spear. As he plunged it into the heart of the beast, it fell to the ground, dead.

The disturbing images melted away and in their place the picture from the Scripture book he'd seen long ago appeared before Naibei's eyes. He sat up and began to shake and cry loudly.

"What happened, man? Are you sick?" his wife asked her distraught husband. *Did he poison himself when drunk?* she wondered.

Finally Naibei calmed down enough to talk. "Jesus, the Good Shepherd of that picture, has come to me." He realized God had used the dream to tell him that he was unable to overcome "the wild beast of alcoholism" in his own strength. But with the sword given him by his father—a picture of God's Word—he had killed the beast. "God has spoken to me," he concluded.

Today God speaks to Naibei in his heart language. Instead of drinking from a bottle each day, there on the slopes of Mt. Elgon, he sits outside his house and drinks in God's words from his Sabaot New Testament.

Sitting before her fireplace in Michigan, Louise praises God for His gift that enables her to express His Word visually. "Some who will not read the words of Scripture respond to a visual expression of the Word of God," she says.

PRAYER

Thank you, God, for your gifts of creativity and skills. May your children thus gifted use their talents for your glory. Pray that as Naibei leads Bible studies for his people, many will find the Good Shepherd through his witness and reading God's Word for themselves. Pray for Louise as she uses her gift of art to glorify God.

MEDITATION

See, I have chosen Bezalel [and Louise] and I have filled [them] with the Spirit of God, with skill, ability and knowledge ... to make artistic designs . . . (Exodus 31:2-4)

For the Lord God says: I will search and find my sheep. I will be like a shepherd looking for his flock. I will ... rescue them from all the places they were scattered in that dark and cloudy day. (Ezekiel 34:11–12, TLB)

REFLECTION

Have I buried my talent in the ground or am I using it for God's glory as the Chinese printer, Naibei and Louise do?

_____

[1] Formerly with Wycliffe, Louise Bass and her husband served 20 years in Papua New Guinea. After her husband's death in 1979, she came home to the U.S. and worked as an artist to put her three children through college. Today, she creates note cards with her art work and inspirational sayings. E-mail BassL@juno.com or visit ReadingUp.com to order.

23

Prepared for the Pass

I want to know one thing—the way to heaven; how to land safe on that happy shore . . . He hath written it down in a book. O give me that book!
—**John Wesley**

In the late 1930s Xinuwa[1] died. But, as he was being prepared for burial, he sat up—alive!

A few weeks later, Xinuwa called his Palikur people together. "Listen to my story. After I died, I walked along a narrow path. And . . . somehow I knew it would take me to our Creator. On both sides of the path, flames of fire leaped up, so I walked right down the middle."

Xinuwa now spoke quickly and ended his story with sadness in his voice. "After a short time I met a man. 'Go back!' he said. 'And don't come again until you have a pass.' I know we Palikur need a pass from the Indian agent to leave the reservation and go to the towns of the civilizados. But a pass to go to God's town? I wanted so much to see God, but I had no pass. I began to cry. Then I woke up."

The people discussed Xinuwa's story.

"Since my walk on that narrow path, I've thought a lot," Xinuwa continued. "And now I understand why we can't go to God's place. It's because He is good and we aren't. He doesn't want us to steal or get angry and fight and kill. God wants us to be good like He is and He wants us to honor Him alone."

The people listened intently. "We'll change! We'll do only good things," they vowed.

They all tried to change. They tried very, very hard—and they changed. For about two weeks. Then, back to feuding and fighting, the same as before.

After Xinuwa died and came alive again, for over 30 years his people told and retold his story. And they always wondered, *What kind of a pass was that man talking about? How can we get it?*

For thousands of years, the Palikur have lived on scattered islands-of-jungle in an everglade of the Amazon basin. There they lived in fear—fear of their neighbors, fear of evil spirits who, they believed, inhabited the rainforests. In the past, this group numbered in the hundreds of thousands. But slave raiders, disease, intergroup warfare, alcohol abuse and violent feuds had decimated the group. In 1965, when a Wycliffe family, Harold and Diana Green, along with their two young sons, went to Brazil to live among the Palikur, they numbered only 800.

"The men spent most of their time lying around in the mud, drunk," Harold says. "We wondered, *Have we come too late?*" The Greens had no idea that the question uppermost in the minds of these people was: *How can we get the pass that will take us to God?*

After living two years among the Palikur and studying their language and culture, the Greens were ready to translate the first verse from God's Word. They chose John 14:6, Jesus' claim that "I am the way, the truth, and the life! Without me, no one can go to the Father."

When the Palikur heard this, they exclaimed, "Jesus must be the *Pass* we've waited for all these years! He is the *Pass* that will take us to God."

Within the next two years, a majority of the Palikur turned to the Lord. Rejoicing that Jesus had forgiven their sins, they began to value forgiveness above revenge. Feuding families met together and publicly forgave one another. "It was better than the Hatfields and the McCoys making up," Diana says.

The people decided to form one large village where they could live together in love, learn God's Word and follow His teachings. Today the Palikur remain a strong, united group and the population has doubled.

"God prepared the Palikur for the coming of His Word almost as well as He prepared the people of Israel by giving them the law. Xinuwa was their Moses," the Greens say. "They knew that though God was holy, they were sinners. The Palikur people had demonstrated to themselves that no matter how hard they tried, they could not be good enough to merit a pass that would enable them to go into the presence of the Holy One. The Word[2] in their heart language ended their search and presented to them the *Pass*—freely given despite their sin."

PRAYER

Praise God that He prepared the Palikur people for His Word! Pray that the Palikur church will remain strong and united as Christians feed on the New Testament, published in 1983. Pray for the Greens and the team of Palikur men now translating the Old Testament and preparing to record the New Testament on audio CDs.

MEDITATION

Listen to me, you islands [-of-jungle]; hear this, you distant nations: Before [you were] born, the Lord called [you] … (Isaiah 49:1)

"I am the way [the Pass] . . . Without me, no one can go to the Father. (John 14:6, CEV)

REFLECTION

As I look back on my life, can I see how God prepared me for the *Pass*?

---

[1]Xinuwa is pronounced She-new-wa.

[2]The Palikur New Testament was published by Bible League in 1983.

24
"Who Could Erase My Record?"

We lived doing evil, not knowing what God's Word said. Today we can see because we can read His Word in our own language.
— Juan, co-translator of the Macuna New Testament, Brazil

Spike calls himself "the black sheep" of his family. "My parents and my seven brothers and sisters and even my relatives at one time banned me from coming inside their houses. My father, frustrated by my criminal activities, once told a policeman, 'Kill him! He's no longer my son.' "

This black sheep, now one of God's sheep, is translating the Bible for his Baluhu people. The path that led Spike[1] to this work is soaked with blood—the blood of people he killed.

Spike continues, "When only 12, I joined one of many youth gangs in our city. From there I was drawn into drugs." The companion of Spike's drug use soon followed: robbery, sometimes with murder as an aside. "At age 15 I served my first prison stint— the first of four by the time I was 19."

Due to the influence of Spike's cousin, known as the "Crime Buster" of the city where Spike's family lived, Spike never spent more than a few months at any one time in prison.

"One of the most traumatic experiences of my life occurred when I was 15 years old," Spike says. His gang members and members of a rival gang met at a disco and fighting erupted. "Pete, leader of this other gang, and I grew up together. We were best friends. That evening, he stabbed me in the back with an ice pick— not just once but twice. Then he ran away, leaving me with the pick in my back. And my gang deserted me. I thought, *This is it. I'm going to die.*"

Searing anger permeated his whole being as he struggled to pull out the pick. That anger motivated him to vow to himself, *No way will I die! I'll live and I'll kill Pete.*

Months later the opportunity came. "I was downtown and saw Pete from a distance. *Here's my chance* . . . I pulled out my 38 revolver and shot. For seven months I evaded the police. I felt like a scampering rat running from a pack of hungry cats."

Spike later learned that the police warrant for his arrest read "attempted murder." His revenge would have to wait.

"People told me, 'If you live by weapons, you'll die by them.' But I vowed I'd kill anyone first who tried to kill me. Pete's gang members were high on my hit list. One night I heard that four of them were in a nearby disco. Our gang burst into the room and sprayed them with gunshot. Before we escaped, I made sure all were dead."

Despite his life of violence, Spike managed to complete high school. On more than one occasion he promised his father he would change. *Why can't I refuse the calling of evil?* he sometimes asked himself. "The pull toward evil is like the influence of drugs. Each time I promised my father I'd go straight, an evil voice would whisper to me, *Follow me. I'll provide you with all the drugs you want. Your life will be full of excitement.* And I'd follow."

After Spike's fourth time in prison, his cousin realized something had to be done or the police would kill Spike. "Become my personal body guard," he offered. *Surely that will provide the excitement my young cousin craves*, he thought.

"Thanks . . . but what I'd really like to do is continue my studies." Spike turned to his father, "Father, will you help me do that?"

His father turned his back on his son without answering. Stung by his father's lack of confidence in him, Spike vowed, *This time I will change!* His mother's words, "My son, as long as I'm alive, I will help you," gave Spike courage to fulfill that promise—for a few years at least. He channeled his energy into studying.

"I would have been completely happy at University, but my creditors were pressuring me. I sat in classes and battled with an almost overpowering thought: *Rob a store and your troubles are over.*"

God had other plans for this seeking-to-go-straight black sheep. A letter from his father, postmarked from the capital city, read: "Son, I'm here working. My boss wants to hire you to keyboard material onto a computer."

"That was more than I could have imagined. These hands of

mine, stained by the blood of a dozen or more people, would be working in an office. I didn't question what I'd be keyboarding. I just knew all would be well—because my father was there."

Spike found that his employer, Don Hannon, was with Wycliffe. "I was keyboarding Scripture in my Baluhu language. Jesus' claims in John 14 blew my mind. He called God His Father! He even claimed He and God were one. 'No one comes to the Father except through me . . . Anyone who has seen me has seen the Father . . .' "

Day after day Spike pondered this new information. "*It was so simple. By believing Jesus, anyone can know God as Father. Are these things true or are they lies?* I wondered. As I keyboarded, God's words were softening my 'wooden' heart. I learned I was guilty before God. I also learned that Jesus didn't condemn me. He wanted to forgive me of my terrible sins!"

Jesus' teaching in Luke 6:27–36 baffled Spike. "*Love your enemies? Is there anyone alive who can do that?* I had learned that if someone slaps you, you slap him back—with a gun. If someone stones you, you stone him—with bigger stones. Pray for my enemies? Yes, I prayed for them: 'Help me find a way to kill them!' "

His attempts to discuss these new ideas with his father were rebuffed. "Keep working, stop asking questions," his father commanded. "Pay no attention to the words."

Spike's questions grew, but he stopped verbalizing them. Things were going well between father and son until—*Having a wife would help my son straighten out his life*, his father decided. Without consulting Spike, he arranged a marriage for him. But the day after the wedding the new bride left to go overseas. "I resented my father trying to control my life," Spike says.

A few months after his bride left, Spike, in further rebellion, had an affair with a cousin, and was dismissed from work. For weeks, his close-knit family members argued. Not knowing that Spike was legally married, some insisted he must marry his cousin. The stress caused Spike to revert to his old lifestyle.

But Don Hannon was not ready to give up on Spike. Don had returned from a year in his home country. He and Latif Anderson, an SIM[2] missionary, set about organizing a team to dub the *JESUS* film into Baluhu. Spike's father reacted favorably to Don's request for his son to be part of that team. "I looked forward to working with Don again," Spike says. "Here was my chance to learn more about Jesus.

"As I read the part of one of the thieves on the cross, I heard Jesus say, 'You will be with me in paradise.' I felt He was talking to me. I had not put my faith in Him, but I knew He had just promised to save me."

The dubbing finished and Spike continued to ponder Jesus' claims. Two years later Ron Johnston, a new SIM missionary, approached Spike. "I need someone to help me learn Baluhu. Would you teach me your language?"

"Over the years, I had worked with missionaries for months at a time." Spike comments. "Though I had read and even translated parts of God's Word, still I had not become a believer. But the attitude of Christians impressed me. Now, as I taught Ron, I observed that same attitude. *I want to commit my life to Jesus Christ*, I concluded."

And he did—but secretly, because he feared his father.

The time came for Ron to leave the city. "I had committed my life to Jesus, but had never learned how to pray," Spike says. "Though Ron had been like a father to me, I hadn't told him I was a believer. *Who will help me so I don't revert to my old way of life?* I cried out in my spirit."

Ron put Spike in contact with another missionary and Spike told him his fears. "Join a group of us for a twice-weekly Bible study," the missionary suggested. At that study, Spike met more members of his new "family."

"I told them about Pete, my best friend, now my enemy. They prayed with me. God replaced my spirit of revenge with a spirit of forgiveness. In my heart I added, *Please, God, reconcile me with Pete.*"

It came time for Spike's educational board exams. "I was frightened," Spike says. "To take those I needed a police clearance from my hometown."

"Don't go to the police station. You'll never get a clearance from the police," relatives warned.

"I was desperate. I considered cutting off my thumbs so they couldn't fingerprint me. But I remembered that my new family was praying for me."

God prompted a friend to give Spike the verses from the Gospel of John 16:22–23, TLB:

You will rejoice; and no one can rob you of that joy. At that time you won't need to ask me for anything, for you can go directly to the Father and ask him, and he will give you what you ask for because you use my name.

"Even though I was terrified," Spike confesses, "I prayed in Jesus' name that God would grant my request. I entered the police station trembling with fear. I left trembling with excitement! In my hands I held my clearance papers. *How can this be? Who could have erased my record?* I hadn't believed God did miracles—until then." Over one hundred people took the exams that same day. Of the seven who passed, Spike was in the top three.

Downtown a year later, Spike suddenly saw Pete walking toward him. "I panicked. *This is the man I almost killed. Will he take revenge?* I bowed my head and began to pray. As he drew closer, his hands reached out toward me. I froze, thinking, *He's going to attack*!"

But as Pete reached Spike, Pete's arms went around him. "My friend, forgive me for what I did," Pete said.

The two, now brothers in Christ, sat in a restaurant and exchanged stories of—what else?—how God had erased the record of their sin!

"It was a miracle that my police record was erased. But the greater miracle," Spike testifies, "is that my sin record was erased. Before I knew Jesus, I was full of pride. Now I kneel in humility before God, and I pray that my enemies also may find new life in Jesus. I was full of evil spirits. Now the Holy Spirit lives in me."

PRAYER

Praise you, Father, that you are able to wipe out our sin-records. Many years ago, after translating Romans 10:14 and 15, Spike said, "How can my Baluhu people call on the One they have not believed in? And how can they believe in the One of whom they have not heard? They can't until they have God's Word in Baluhu!" Pray for Spike as he recently began translation of John's Gospel. Pray that Spike's family and others in the community will read and respond to portions of the Word now available in Baluhu. Having returned to his former community, Spike asks for prayer "that our family will be a witness in a place where no believers have ever before lived."

MEDITATION

We had to celebrate and be glad, because this brother ... was dead and is alive again; he was lost and is found. (Luke 15:32)

He forgave us all our sins, having canceled the written code ... that was against us ... nailing it to the cross. (Colossians 2:13–14)

REFLECTION

Have I asked God to erase my record of sin against Him?

---

[1]Spike is a pseudonym, as are all names of people in this story.

[2]SIM (Serving in Mission), which was formerly known as Sudan Interior Mission, now includes the ministries of Africa Evangelical Fellowship and Andes Evangelical Mission.

25

The Word Made Real through Drama

God yearns to touch minds and hearts with His life-changing message . . .
Therefore, His Word must often go beyond the printed page to other media
such as . . . drama. [These] non-print media . . . pique spiritual interest
and establish a bridge for oral cultures to understand the Word of God.
— **JAARS Vernacular Media Services brochure**

"I remember sitting in the encroaching darkness on a low stool around an open fire—my first Christmas in Ghana, my first Christmas away from my homeland," Carol says.

That was 1972. Dean and Carol Jordan, Wycliffe translators, had been living in a Nafana village since the previous March— interacting with the people, learning their language and culture.

"That Christmas is one of my treasured memories of living in Africa," Carol says. "Ma Fatima, the village pastor's wife, served up portions of *fufu* and *funumu* soup—calabash seed sauce over pounded yam. She had spent her whole day preparing it." A Nafana hostess always makes sure she has enough for the extended family and guests, seldom less than 20 people. Carol was impressed with Fatima's careful art in apportioning out servings. The husband and male guests were served first, then children. Women guests were served next. And last, the women who had cooked and served the food.

"With an ankle-length native cloth stretched tightly over my knees, I sat and dipped my fingers in a common bowl with the other women. As I ate their food, I had a deep sense of belonging. A wonderful contentment settled over me. Yes, this is where the Lord wants us."

A treasured memory. Yet for Carol, another Christmas in West Africa stands out even more—the year the Nafana people read mimeographed copies of the Christmas story in their language. And young people dramatized that timeless story!

"Dean and I—enthralled—sat in a tiny, mud-walled church," Carol says, recalling memories as vivid as though they happened only yesterday. "The small room and the meager props provided lots of opportunity for imagination. In order to turn the bare sanctuary into a bustling Bethlehem, every young person played a role. Even the curious onlookers fit unwittingly into the scene. No need for costumes. The traditional Nafana dress served well. Small goats and sheep roamed about lending a pastoral ambiance. Rough, backless pews marked off the stable with its Treasure. A woman's wraparound cloth suspended from a beam defined the makeshift stable door.

"The play began with shepherds entering by a side door," Carol continues. "They wandered up and down the short aisle till they came to the stable. Shalom, our pet lamb, cuddled in a shepherd's arms, gave credence to this actor's role in the play. His proud owners laughed when he obligingly 'baa-ed' as if on cue.

"The young shepherd-actors approached the stable door and to announce their coming, in Nafana tradition, called out, 'Kau-Kau!' Joseph came to the door. 'May we see the *nmgaa shofun Kristo wre* (the life-giving Christ)?' a shepherd asked.

"Then, at Joseph's raised eyebrows, he explained that while he and his companions were watching sheep on a hillside just outside town, *bitumblo* (messengers) appeared in the night sky. The *bitumblo*, they said, told them to go into town and they'd find the Messiah in a stable. Peering over Joseph's shoulder, the shepherd-actor added, 'The *bitumblo* said the Messiah would be sleeping in a feed-trough.'

"Joseph pulled back the cloth stable door. He looked off into the night, then back at the shepherds. 'Tell me once again what you saw,' he said, as though he couldn't believe what he'd heard. While the shepherds repeated their story, Joseph led them to where his young wife lay on a bed of straw cradling her Baby.

"The wide-eyed wonderment of the young actor portraying Joseph and the awe with which he presented Mary and the Christ Child opened my eyes. God's Word dramatized in such a natural, unsophisticated setting caused me to understand the reality of the incarnation. I understood a little more about Christ's humanity—and also Joseph's. Did Joseph have lingering doubts about this Child born to his wife? If so, these God-sent shepherds surely calmed any nagging questions he had regarding who this Baby really was."

171

As Carol watched the drama, she concluded that "The mighty God we serve went to great lengths to impress on Joseph His truth: this Child truly was the Messiah, the long-awaited one. And Joseph was given the ministry and privilege of watching over Him for a short time.

"That night I was impressed, first, that I served the same God Joseph served; second, that this new missionary had a lot to learn from these unsophisticated people. And I was confident that in the years to come God would dispel doubts, which would inevitably arise regarding our ministry among the Nafana."

In the years following that memorable Christmas, the Jordans facilitated the translation of the Nafaanra New Testament and it was published by the International Bible Society. The Jordans saw it dedicated in 1985. A community-appointed committee of Nafana men is now translating the Old Testament. The committee works under the auspices of a national organization, the Ghana Institute of Linguistics, Literacy and Bible Translation (GILLBT),[1] until recently directed by Justin Frempong, now under Mrs. Georgina Quaisie's direction.

The Jordans now live in North Carolina in a duplex shared with Carol's mother, Mary Schmitt, who along with her late husband has long supported missions. For a few months each year, Dean does exegetical consulting with the men on the translation committee as these men continue checking Scripture for accuracy and clarity.

PRAYER

Praise God that He teaches us through those whom He sends us to minister to. Pray that the Nafana believers will continue to grow strong as they read the New Testament in their heart language. Praise God for the faithfulness of the men on the translation committee, and pray for strength and wisdom for them and Dean as they work on the Old Testament. Pray for continued strength for Carol as she ministers to the committee men and joyfully tends to her mother's needs.

MEDITATION

Generation after generation stands in awe of your work; each one tells stories of [and dramatizes] your mighty acts. (Psalm 145:4, MSG)

Then, in that time there were some sheep-looking-after people (shepherds) and they were sleeping out in the bush with their sheep. And the messenger of the Big God of the sky went and showed himself to them. And the Big God's shining (glory) caused the place to shine brightly. And the sky messenger said to them all, "Don't fear! Look! This sweet event will be a face-shining (happiness) to all my people. Today our Owner Christ, the Life-saving One, He is born in David's town. You will know that the event you will see is true. You will see that they will wrap the child in a cloth and lay him in a sheep-feeding thing." In an instant! Surprisingly! Many messengers appeared and came to help that other messenger. And they were "giving God a Name" (glorifying God) saying, "The face of that Big God there in heaven is shining (He is happy). And those in the land here whose faces He causes to shine (He is happy with), to them He will give rest (peace)." (Luke 2:8–14, a back-translation from Nafana)

REFLECTION

Is Christmas to me the celebration of the God-made-flesh story? As Christmases come and go, have I lost the awe of that "sweet event" when the "Life-Saving One" was born? If so, how can I regain it?

---

[1]The goal of GILLBT is to see Vision 2025 fulfilled in Ghana. Currently work in over 31 languages is ongoing. New Testaments have been translated into 17 of those languages, and GILLBT works to ensure that this Scripture is used in churches and by individuals.

26
An Authoritative Word

We need no more words, but a Word, an authoritative communication . . . that speaks truth that can set us free. We need what Martin Luther in his famous hymn called "that Word above all earthly powers."
—Dr. Donald W. McCullough

Moguain's brown eyes mirrored his excitement. "Our people need to hear this!"

Moguain is a member of a committee translating the New Testament into Kubo, a language of Papua New Guinea. That morning the committee had worked with Tom Covington, a Bible translator with Pioneers, on a first draft of Acts 8:9–24.

In his excitement over the clarity of God's Word in his heart language, Moguain bravely proclaimed, "Next Sunday I'll preach from this passage."

For more than an hour, even before anyone arrived, the tropical heat had pressed into the metal-roofed church building. And the service had been underway for at least an hour before Moguain rose to preach. Nursing babies, now full and contented, slept in mothers' laps. Toddlers stopped running around; sprawled out on the floor, they too slept. Heads nodded. Older people snored with mouths sagging open, throwing teenagers into fits of giggles, which they tried unsuccessfully to stifle. Even dogs that had ignored owners' "Shush!" slept quietly at their masters' feet. In the audience, buzzing flies seemed to be the only living creatures wide-awake.

It was before this sleepy congregation that Moguain stood up. He read ploddingly—his first attempt to read Kubo Scripture in public. The audience stirred awake! Suddenly those who had settled down for another hour's nap focused their attention on Moguain. The content of the passage made up for what his halting delivery lacked.

From Acts 8:9–24 he read of a man who had gained his position in society by working magic, a man acclaimed by his people as "the divine power known as the Great Power." Magic! The people could identify with that. A man had then been caught up in a people movement to Christ and had "believed and was baptized." Drawn by the power Phillip and the apostles possessed, he followed closely after them. He wanted to regain his former position by tapping into that greater power, and then manipulate God to further his own ends. Peter saw that the man primarily craved power, not Christ, and strongly rebuked him.

This was the story Moguain read to his people in their heart language, the story that had excited him a few days previously. An alert audience followed his every word throughout the lengthy and repetitious[1] sermon.

Moguain barely finished the closing prayer before a heated discussion erupted. An elder stood and shouted above the din, expressing the deep concern the elders have for their congregations. His harsh words shocked the audience into silence. "Anyone who is hiding magic or is involved with evil spirits will be condemned, just as Peter condemned this man."

"The elders know that syncretism—combining Christian beliefs with the beliefs of the people—still exists in the churches," Tom says. "Even some baptized people are still bound by ancestral traditions. Some still fear the spirits and seek to placate them. Some dabble in magic then try to hide this from the church leaders. That story from Acts 8 spoke to the Kubo in a way it hasn't spoken to me or my people for many generations. Once again I saw that God's Word continues to speak to the problems and sins of each culture. That morning, God's Word—an authoritative Word—brought the problem of the Kubo church out into the light."

PRAYER

Pray that portions of the New Testament will continue to speak to believers bringing freedom from ancestral practices. The local church is now taking responsibility for finishing the translation of the New Testament. Pray for unity and wisdom for the translation committee, and pray for Tom as he finds time to assist them.

MEDITATION

They will be my people, and I will be their God. I will give them singleness of heart and action, so that they will always fear me for their own good and the good of their children after them. (Jeremiah 32:38–39)

"Therefore come out from them and be separate," says the Lord. "Touch no unclean thing, and I will receive you." (2 Corinthians 6:17)

REFLECTION

Has God's authoritative Word pointed out any syncretism in my life? Do I try to hold on to worldly ways with one hand and hold on to Jesus' ways with the other?

---

[1]The grammar of some Papua New Guinea languages requires a lot of repetition, an aspect found in many oral languages.

God's Word Brought Light

Understanding comes not from people's opinions—but from the Lord through His Word and the ministry of His Spirit to our hearts . . . The Word is our greatest source of understanding.

—Darlene Foster

"Our million-dollar view was absolutely wonderful—once we arrived. But that 7,000-foot climb to the village perched atop a mountain wasn't much fun!"

Haga, a Yagaria village in Papua New Guinea, was home to Carol Gutwein and Donna McKibben, Bible translators with New Tribes Mission.[1] After being away for a long period, late one afternoon the women had once again mastered the upward trek. Mountain night chill would soon envelop them, so they scurried around to make their house-in-the-clouds livable. A roaring fire in the wood burning stove would warm their bodies as well as their spirits. The wick on the kerosene refrigerator had to be lit. "People always asked, 'How does that fire make things cold?' And I sure didn't know," Carol confesses.

Spider webs must be swept down. "Let's see, where did we store the broom? I'll sweep down the cobwebs and then . . . Wait!" Carol interrupted herself. "First we have to pay the young people for carrying our supplies up the mountain. When we left here, where'd you put the money, Donna?"

"I didn't move it."

"It's not here. Where could it have gone?"

Carol and Donna searched thoroughly. But a slit in one of the plastic window coverings—just large enough for a hand to reach through and unhook the window lock—was all they found. Someone had crawled through that window. The money was gone. Stolen!

Heartsick, they called Jonah, a village elder whose life had been transformed from a proud village warrior to a humble and dedicated servant of God. It was because of him that the women had chosen to live in Haga. He had taken responsibility for looking out for these two "red girls" from the very first. Although Jonah had lived most of his life never having heard of Jesus, his speech was now filled with talk about Him. "Jesus is preparing a place for me! I'm so glad I'm Heaven-bound," he often proclaimed. And he was always citing answers to prayer. *Well*, Carol thought, *now's an opportunity for Jonah to pray with us and see God answer.*

"Lord, help us find out who took that money," Jonah prayed. "Get it back to my two red daughters. And give the culprits a just penalty." Suddenly, just after Jonah pronounced his "Amen," he turned to the women with what he considered an inspiration.

"I know a sorcerer who's really good in such cases as this. He finds names of people who've stolen things. Let's go see him," Jonah urged. "He's powerful!"

"Jonah, our father, what do you think the source of this man's power is?" Carol tactfully asked. "Is his power just *human* power?"

"Oh no, Kalo," Jonah quickly answered, pronouncing her name in Yagaria, "it's supernatural." He then admitted he'd never thought about the source of the power. "He works *lusa*, not *nalisa*. *Nalisa* kills people. *Lusa* makes it rain when our crops are about to die. It heals sick people . . . Yep, this man's a *lusa* sorcerer. He does good, so his power must come from God," Jonah concluded.

"Is he a believer?" Carol asked.

No, Jonah admitted, he wasn't, but still "the power must be from God" was his final word.

Eventually, those who had taken the money were found and punished. "Not through *lusa*," Carol says. "Jonah still maintained that *lusa* sorcerers received power from God because, 'they do so much good.' It was impossible to convince him otherwise. He knew!

The women continued studying the Yagaria language and culture—and they fervently prayed for Jonah. The day came when Carol and Yagaria speakers began Bible translation. "After translating the Gospel of Mark and some of Genesis, we started Acts. Excited about having God's Word in his language, Jonah often came and listened to newly translated portions. I remember the day we read the story in Acts 16 of the fortunetelling girl with a spirit of divination," Carol says.

Suddenly it was clear to Jonah. "Now I understand. Even though those men thought that girl did good for them, the spirit in her was not from God. It was a demon giving her power. And that's why Paul commanded it to go. That's just like the spirits give our *lusa* people power. Even though we think they do good, their power comes from Satan!" Jonah became as emphatic on his new position as he had been on his old position. Impatiently, he argued with others who didn't yet see this truth.

"Jonah, our father, do what we did," Carol gently urged. "Pray and trust God to make them understand through His Word, and stop arguing with them."

"God, bring understanding to my people just as you did to me," he often prayed.[2] And he stopped arguing.

"Praise God how He uses His Word when we work together," Carol says as she concludes Jonah's story. "The New Testament was published in 1975. I'm so thankful for all who had input into getting God's Word to Jonah and his people—churches and people who prayed and sent money. And help from other missions—for instance, Wycliffe. As a translator and now as a consultant, I don't know where I'd be without the help of SIL. All New Tribes translators use the exegetical helps, including Translator's Workplace, produced by SIL. Through the years I've profited from attending SIL workshops. And the entire Yagaria New Testament was consultant checked by SIL linguists.

"God's Word brings light—and that light travels faster when Christians cooperate!"

PRAYER

Praise God that many hundreds of Yagaria people now believe in the One who brings light and understanding. Praise God that Jonah was humble enough to admit he was wrong. Pray that God will use His Word to bring light to believers who do not yet understand about *lusa* power. Pray for Carol as she makes trips back to help the Yagaria people revise the New Testament, prepare Bible study curriculum, revise literacy materials, and continue Old Testament translation.

MEDITATION

The unfolding of your words gives light; it gives understanding to the simple. (Psalm 119:130)

He [the Spirit] gives . . . the ability to know whether it is really the Spirit of God or another spirit that is speaking. (1 Corinthians 12:10, NLT)

REFLECTION

Once God brings light to some dark area of my thinking, am I impatient and critical of other believers who don't yet see the truth? Or do I "pray and trust God and stop arguing" as Jonah did?

---

[1]Carol, now Carol Gutwein Kaptain, is with New Tribes and until recently, lived with her husband, Chuck, at the SIL Center in Papua New Guinea. Chuck, with Wycliffe, served in the Center Radio Department. They recently moved to the New Tribes Center in Sanford, Florida. Donna, now Donna McKibben Plett, is no longer with New Tribes.

[2]In 1968, Jonah was already old and frail by the standards of his culture. Still, he lived another 35 years, longer than many of his peers and also longer than most of his children and grandchildren. His vibrant testimony remained strong and bright to the end.

28

The Deaf Will Hear

In that day the deaf will hear the words of the scroll . . .

— **Isaiah the prophet (29:18)**

"I got goose bumps," wrote Mrs. Kato. "I felt like the Word of God was coming alive right in front of me as I watched it."

Mrs. Kato, one of Japan's Deaf,[1] had just watched a video of the book of Acts in Japanese Sign Language (JSL). "I wanted to watch the whole thing again. But my pastor uses it for prayer meetings, so I needed to return it." Her letter goes on to state that the JSL Bible was "much, much easier" to understand than her Japanese Bible. "It was as though someone had been there and was telling me the story. I want to hear it again and again. But I don't want to just hear the Word, pray, and be done with it. I want to tell others."

After years in an abusive marriage, Mrs. Kato is now a single mother, raising four children alone. But she knows she is not really alone because Jesus came into her life. He has filled her with His Spirit and placed her in a community—the Christian community of the Deaf in Japan.

Near the end of her letter, Mrs. Kato writes a prayer to the God she's only recently come to know: "Thank you, God, that Jesus died on the cross to atone for my sin. He was raised on the third day. If Jesus didn't exist, we would be in darkness." Then her letter emits a stream of praise: "I'm so thankful! I'm thrilled that in the name of Jesus we can meet with God the Father. I give joy-filled thanks to Heaven!"

This joy-filled letter was addressed to Mark Penner. In 1993, Mark helped start the Japan Deaf Evangel Mission (J-DEM).[2] That same year, Mark and a team of Japanese Deaf people, including a Deaf linguist, began translating God's Word into JSL.[3] "We named the project ViBi—Video Bible. Our goal at ViBi is 'The Living Word in a Living Deaf Community.' We're not expecting to meet that goal alone. The General Director of The Japan Bible Society, Rev. Watabe, serves on our board. And JBS recently launched a funding campaign to make the completion of the ViBi translation a possibility in the next 15 years."

Further cooperation comes from Southern Baptist missionaries in Japan. "We thank God that Nan Jordan and other Southern Baptist missionaries were willing right from the start to take on the ViBi translation project with us," Mark says.

Mark and his wife Mary Esther, both MKs (missionary kids), grew up in Japan and had a burden to reach the Deaf. They returned to Japan with WorldVenture. Though Mark became fluent in Japanese fairly quickly, he says, "On the other hand, JSL was a totally new language for me."

Besides the book of Acts, the Gospel of Mark, four of the New Testament Epistles and two Old Testament books have been translated into JSL. And in early 2000 Mark wrote friends: "Great news! Three thousand copies of the *JESUS* video JSL Version will be ready for distribution in early December." Today those videos are reaching people who would never read a Bible or watch a JSL Bible video.

Mr. Uta[4] is one of those people. After viewing the JSL *JESUS* video, he e-mailed Mark: "I've never had an interest in the Bible before. This is the first time I've seen a story about Christ in sign language. I would like to order The Gospel of Mark and Sign Worship Workshop videos."

A hearing pastor from Hokkaido in northern Japan attended a class to learn JSL so he could better work alongside the Deaf. "Last week, I loaned my teacher the JSL *JESUS* video," he reported. "Though she took the video reluctantly, at the next class she said she was impressed with the clear and understandable signing. She told me she cried when they nailed Jesus to the cross. As we talked, she repeated the JSL sign for 'death' and 'resurrection,' over and over."

The Deaf will hear! And the Deaf in Japan are hearing through ViBi's ministry.

PRAYER

Praise God that missions in Japan are cooperating, working alongside the Deaf as they reach out to their own. The result is that more among the Deaf community are turning to Christ. Thank God for Campus Crusade, the Southern Baptist Japan Deaf Team, and others who distribute JSL *JESUS* videos. Mark requests, "Pray for even closer cooperation between Deaf and hearing Christians in this crucial program." Ted Bergman, SIL's International Survey Coordinator, says, "When we do surveys and start translation projects among the Deaf, God uses His Word to transform lives for His glory." Ask the Lord of the harvest to call workers to do surveys in sign languages.

MEDITATION

Jesus told them, "Go back … and tell what you have heard and seen—the blind see, the lame walk, the lepers are cured, the deaf hear … " (Matthew 11:4–5, NLT)

People were overwhelmed with amazement. "He [Jesus] has done everything well," they said. "He even makes the deaf hear . . ." (Mark 7:37)

REFLECTION

The Deaf include people of every nationality, living in every country of the world, using many different sign languages. And Deaf communities worldwide almost always have a much smaller percentage of Christians than other communities of the country. What can I do to help provide God's Word for the Deaf?

---

[1]The Deaf Community of Japan consists of approximately 250,000 people.

[2]J-DEM is chaired by Rev. Matsumoto, a former translator with ViBi and now pastor of the Yamagata Deaf Church that Mrs. Kato attends.

[3]Mark studied linguistics at an SIL school when on a furlough and has continued his linguistic studies since. Today, a Japanese man named Shiguru with an MA in linguistics heads up the ViBi translation program.

[4]Uta is a pseudonym.

29

One Life at a Time

We need to be committed to giving forth His Word—to the multitudes or to the ones and twos. When we are, we see a simple truth in operation: God uses ordinary people to do extraordinary things. He's not looking for great ability, but great availability.

—Rev. Coleman Tyler

"Whew! It's humid!"

On an October night in 1999, more than one person made that remark. But despite the Brazilian heat and humidity, anticipation was high on the Logos II, an Operation Mobilization (OM) ministry ship. Docked in the port of Recife, the ship was being prepared for Operation Unload. Trucks carrying five huge containers filled with books were to arrive at the dock in the wee hours of the morning. The books—Bible teaching and other educational material—would eventually find their place in West Africa among French and English speakers.

The ship's multinational community of 200 men, women and children scurried around making sure that by 3 a.m. everything and everyone would be ready to move the cargo. One million books!

That would triple the number already on board. A crew of 30 had been recruited to begin the heave-ho work of unloading and getting the heavy boxes aboard. Seventy more would join them at 7 a.m. Then a one-hundred-strong human chain, stretching from containers to ship's holds, would relay those thousands of boxes.

"If all goes as planned, we'll pull away from the quayside by 4 p.m.," the ship's captain announced.

Why was Logos II in Recife? "On a recent Sunday afternoon, over 6,000 people were waiting to visit the ship," says Coleman Tyler. An Episcopalian pastor from the U.S., Tyler was serving in the interdenominational mission context of OM. "Much of the ship's ministry involves reaching the multitudes," Tyler says.

The Tylers, with their three children, were on board the Logos II for over a year. Tyler served as the ship's pastor and personnel director. In their second year of ministry on the Logos, he was appointed director of the ship. Susan, whose main ministry is always wife and mother, taught family and marriage seminars with her husband. For a time, she was involved in the ship's Sports Outreach Ministry, as well as in evangelizing and encouraging national believers. Twelve-year-old Matthew made his parents proud when he enthusiastically signed up for that early morning Operation Unload crew.

Recife—what a place to minister to the masses and to be ministered to! Pastor Tyler reported that "the dynamic Anglican-Episcopal Diocese brims with warm and inviting evangelical faith. The church's three Sunday services pack 700 to 800 people in each service. Bishop Cavalcanti extended a gracious welcome to the ship's entire community. Because of this godly man, many doors of ministry opened to us."

In Recife, Pastor Tyler was also invited by Pastor Miguel Uchoa to preach at the Church of the Holy Spirit. "A congregation of around 800 people—mostly young families—worships God there each Sunday. Planted just over three years ago, it meets in a former nightclub complex called Babylon," Tyler reported. Yes, "Babylon has fallen" and today a "New Jerusalem" of praise meets in that building!

But it's not only the masses and the megachurches that the ship's crew members are interested in. "The humble Anglican Pentecostal Mission in one of Recife's 450 slum areas stands in contrast to prominent city churches," Tyler says. "My family and I spent a morning with Pastor Jardson. Sewage trickles down parched hillsides. Running water is available only once a week at four locations. In this less-than-desirable place where he's chosen to live with his family, Pastor Jardson is the incarnation of Christ to the hillside dwellers. He and his family live there at risk to their lives from local drug lords, disease and poverty. But amid the sadness and pain, I saw signs of God's grace and glory."

Then there was Aparicio—one of thousands who visited the Logos II in Recife. "I was on the quayside welcoming people standing in a long queue. In broken Portuguese, I talked with Aparicio, a young Romanian man who spoke five languages. I invited him on board to meet Joe, our one Romanian crew member.

Now, was that just a coincidence or was it divine Providence?" Pastor Tyler says. And his smile tells you that he believes it was divine Providence.

"I believe in God, but I've always wondered if I could truly be His friend," Aparicio told Joe.

Joe assured him from the Word that he could know God through Jesus, and Aparicio invited Jesus into his life. He left the dock with a Romanian Bible tucked under his arm and the assurance that God was his Friend—One who will talk to him through that Bible in his heart language.

Aparicio returned to the ship twice. "I've visited an Anglican church and I want to begin going there," he told Tyler.

Indeed, at the dock in Recife, the crew of the Logos II had faced a daunting task. *Will we be able to accomplish Operation Unload in just a scant 12 hours? Will we have the ship ready by tomorrow afternoon for its nine-day Trans-Atlantic voyage to Ghana?* Enthusiasm, excitement, joy, purpose, cooperation, hard work carried the day. The ship left on time!

As the Logos II sailed away, other questions—more connected to bodies than books—were on Pastor Tyler's mind. *Will Aparicio and the hundreds who came to Christ in the three weeks we've docked here continue steadfast? How long before the Anglican Pentecostal Mission will have enough money to purchase a building for the believers to meet in there in the slums?*[1]

As Tyler says, much of the ministry of Logos II is to the multitudes. In the three months the ship was in South America, over 200,000 people climbed the gangways to attend seminars and conferences, and tour the ship. "Some 192,000 books went forth—over half of them Bibles and books on the Bible."

Many who visit Logos ships hear the life-changing message of the Gospel for the first time. And many tell stories of sadness, and are individually prayed with. "Yes, we reach the multitudes," Tyler says. "Yet at the heart of the ministry is commitment to individuals—one life at a time."

Epilogue

As the Logos II crossed the Atlantic, it charted the same course, in reverse, sailed by slave-traders for 250 years. It first docked in Tema, Ghana, "the Gateway to Africa." In the first four weeks there, over 110,000 people walked up the ship's gangways. The slave traders' vessels took some 10,000 people a year out of Africa into slavery. In contrast, the Logos II brought a message of freedom: Jesus' invitation to "Come to me . . . Keep company with me and you'll learn to live freely . . ." (Matthew 11:28, 30, MSG).

PRAYER

Praise God for the ministry of Logos ships to the multitudes and to individuals. Pray that those who came to know Christ will grow in faith and bear fruit. Pray for the Tyler family. [2]

MEDITATION

Then he calls his friends and neighbors together and says, "Rejoice with me; I have found my lost sheep." I tell you that in the same way there will be . . . rejoicing in heaven over one sinner who repents . . . (Luke 15:6–7)

Greater love has no one than this, that he lay down his life for his friends. You are my friends if you do what I command. (John 15:13–14)

REFLECTION

Have I been called on by God to reach the masses, or to reach individuals in my neighborhood or at my workplace? Whatever my call, am I faithfully fulfilling it?

---

[1] A family in the Church of the Redeemer in Montgomery, Alabama, the Tyler's former parish, provided money for the building.

[2] Coleman Tyler currently pastors an Anglican church in Virginia Beach, Virginia.

30

And Two Brothers from El Tambo Went

Go home to your own people and tell them the great things el Señor has done for you . . .

— Jesus, (Mark 5:19, English translation of the Reina Valera Version, 1960)

It was early 1974 on a Monday morning in Guayaquil, Ecuador. Antonio, a young pastor, came into the office of Southern Baptist missionary Stanley Stamps. He contained his excitement long enough to go through the initial greetings and polite talk. Then he burst out, "Hermano Stanley, yesterday two Quechua men dressed in ponchos walked about ten miles to come to our church! One long braid hung down each man's back—in the same way the Indian men from the Andes wear their hair." His voice rose. "They want a Bible! They want to be baptized! And they want to see you!"

The two men, he said, had left El Tambo, their high-in-the-Andes hometown, and settled in the fertile lowlands to homestead government assigned land. "Jose Maria and Manuel Jesus Pinguil-Loja —that's their names—are brothers. Before they start work, each morning at four, they listen to a gospel broadcast in Spanish on their battery-operated radio. They were convicted of their sin and they understood enough to know they needed Jesus to save them. The radio evangelist said people should find a church that preaches the Gospel, get a Bible and read it, and be baptized. And now," he reiterated, "they want to see you."

And I want to see these men too, Stanley had already decided. That week he drove to Antonio's house and picked him up. Following the two men's instructions, they turned off the highway onto a dusty track that led them through fields and across small streams. At a grove of trees where two split-bamboo houses stood on stilts high above the ground, Stanley blew the horn. Soon two couples appeared from the fields carrying tools. Beaming faces and hearty abrazos from the men welcomed them, and then they were ushered up a notched-pole ladder into one of the houses.

"There I sat with two men from the only province in Ecuador with no evangelical church," Stanley says. "It was rumored that it was unsafe for evangelicals to be caught in that province at night. Even on a day trip through that portion of the Andes, a person might encounter Indians, drunk and staggering along the road."

Antonio and Stanley listened to the men and were convinced they were indeed true *hermanos* (brothers) in the faith. As Stanley pointed out Bible passages for the men to read, he saw their wives climbing up the pole ladder carrying food. "Wow! Was I ever glad to see boiled eggs and hot bread rather than a roasted *cuy*. That small rodent, similar to a guinea pig, is a delicacy to an Andean Indian, but even the thought of one makes my stomach squeamish."

The couples sent their visitors away laden with pineapples, papaya and sugar cane—"first fruits" showing their new faith. The Quechua men were left with a Spanish Bible but Antonio and Stanley knew they needed God's Word in their mother tongue.

On their second visit, they found the brothers as excited to welcome them as the first time. To one, Stanley gave a New Testament. To the other, he gave the book of Romans—Quechua Scripture he had obtained from the Gospel Missionary Union (now Avant Ministries) in Quito. The men immediately opened their books in their mother tongue and began reading as Stanley thumbed through the Spanish Bible left with them. He saw verse after verse underlined with comments written in the margin: "This is true." "I have tried this." "Amen!" "Praise the Lord!"

"Read aloud to us from these books I just gave you," Stanley suggested. Portions from God's Word were read in the melodious Quechua tones. "Every once in a while they'd exclaim in Spanish, 'Oh, Hermano! This is so much easier to understand!' I said to myself, *These two men only recently came to know the Author of this Book. And I have the joy of hearing them read His Word for the very first time in their heart language!* The thrill I felt was equal to none I'd ever experienced."

On Easter Sunday in April 1974 Jose and Manuel[1] were baptized in a small stream near Pastor Antonio's church. A few weeks later, the brothers reported to Stanley, "We've been reading about the demon-possessed man Jesus healed. He wanted to follow Jesus, but Jesus told him, 'No, go home and tell your own people what I've done for you.' We believe Jesus wants us to do that—go home to El Tambo and tell our people about Him."

So they went. That visit resulted in two close relatives coming to know Jesus. And each time the brothers went home, more came to Christ. Within a few months, 16 people became believers.

Archie and Julia Jones, Southern Baptist church planters, began a church in a town near El Tambo. "There's a church nearby," Jose and Manuel told their relatives. The El Tambo believers began walking the eight miles to that "nearby" church to worship with other believers. By October 1975 all the El Tambo believers were baptized.

In their heart language, Jose and Manuel read the Lord's word, "Go home to your own people and tell them the great things el Señor has done for you." And the two brothers from El Tambo went.

PRAYER
Thank you, Father, that you speak to people from Your Word. Praise God that Jose and Manuel obeyed the Holy Spirit's word to them. Pray for a deepening love for one another and for God among the El Tambo believers. Pray the church will follow Jose and Manuel's example and reach out to those who have not heard.

MEDITATION
Then he [Andrew] brought Simon [his brother] to meet Jesus . . . (John 1:42, NLT)

I will praise you, O Lord, with all my heart; I will tell of all your wonders. (Psalm 9:1)

REFLECTION
Do I, like the two brothers from El Tambo, have a concern to tell my family and relatives about what the Lord has done in my life?

---

[1]Among their own people, the Quechua men in this story are referred to by both their first and middle names.

31

Hallelujah, We-e!
Praise the Lord, Wo-o!

It was the moment that epitomizes the goal of a lifetime—seeing a group of people who formerly had no Bible respond in praise to the Living Word.
—John Ellenberger

Cold night winds would soon bring frost to the gardens of the Damal people if the drought continued. The Damal, subsistence farmers living in the Ilaga Valley, Irian Jaya,[1] are dependent on their gardens year round. When first planted, a sweet potato garden needs heavy rains almost daily. But for more than a year, drought had prevailed. Two months had passed since the Valley had seen even a bit of rain, and cloudless skies offered no hope.

Damal pastors and elders had invited John and Helen Ellenberger of The Christian and Missionary Alliance to join them in a valley-wide seminar. This would be the Ellenberger's last time with the Damals before leaving to return to the USA.

Fervent prayer focused on the critical need for life-giving rain—rain that literally meant life and death for their people. Each pastor and elder possessed a copy of the newly printed book of Revelation in their language. The last session had ended with a study from chapters 21 and 22: the vision of the New Jerusalem, heaven, and Jesus' promise that He would come soon. "Even so, come, Greatest Big-man Jesus!" they responded.

Then suddenly, thunder crashed; raindrops pelted down onto the aluminum roof of the church, drowning out even the penetrating song of the forest cicada. It was impossible to hear further teaching or prayers. But that mattered little. That week these pastors had worshiped God, studied His Word, petitioned Him for rain. And now, no thought of muddy trails that all must travel to return home. No bemoaning the pain caused by leeches they would encounter on wet foliage. Rather, a spontaneous breaking forth into worship. Drowning out the noise of the rain, their voices ascended high above the aluminum roof: "Hallelujah, we-e! Praise the Lord, wo-o!"

A bit of heaven came down in that village as Damal men held in their hands the Word of God—a meaningful, life-giving Book. Translation, contextualization, worship all came together as the Ellenbergers heard these Damal men praising God for what the Living Word had done in their lives.

PRAYER

Our Heart

Our heart, our desire,
Is to see the nations worship.
Our cry, our prayer
Is to sing Your praise
To the ends of the earth.
That with one mighty voice
Every tribe and tongue rejoices.
Our heart, our desire,
Is to see the nations worship You! [2]

Father, with the Damal pastors we say, "Hallelujah, we-e! Praise the Lord, wo-o!" Pray that Damal believers will stand strong in rainy seasons as well as in dry seasons.

MEDITATION

And I, John, saw the holy city, new Jerusalem, coming down from God out of heaven, prepared as a bride adorned for her husband. And I heard a great voice out of heaven saying, "Behold, the tabernacle of God is with men, and he will dwell with them … And there shall be no more death, neither sorrow, nor crying, neither shall there be any more pain [nor dry seasons] … " (Revelation 21:2–4, KJV)

205

REFLECTION

How long has it been since I spontaneously broke into praise of "Greatest Big-Man Jesus"? Is my desire "to see the nations worship"?

---

[1]Irian Jaya is the eastern-most province of Indonesia. It shares the island with Papua New Guinea. Once known as Netherlands New Guinea, then West Irian, now it is called Papua.

[2]Integrity Music granted permission to use the words to "Our Heart," George Searcy and John Chisum, 1993 Integrity's Hosanna! Music/ASCAP & Integrity's Praise! Music/BMI.

Appendix A
Websites

American Missionary Fellowship (AMF)
www.amf.org

APCM (see Pioneers International)

Assemblies of God World Missions
www.worldmissions.ag.org

Asia Pacific Christian Mission (APCM)
(see Pioneers of Australia)

Associate Reformed Presbyterian Church,
World Witness
www.worldwitness.org

Avant Minisrries
www.avantministries.org

Baptist General Conference Board of World Missions
www.bgc.world.org

Bible College of Victoria (BCV)
www.bcv.vic.edu.au

Bible College of Victoria (BCV)
Mission Aviation Course
dsearle@bcv.vic.edu.au

Bible Fellowship Church Board of Missions
www.bfcbom.org

Together We Can!

Bible League
www.bibleleague.org

Bible Translation & Literacy (BTL)
www.btlkenya.org

Campus Crusade for Christ International (CCC)
www.ccci.org

Canada Institute of Linguistics (CanIL)
www.canil.ca

Child Evangelism Fellowship (CEF)
www.cefonline.com

The Christian and Missionary Alliance (C&MA)
www.cmalliance.org

Christians in Action Missions International (CinA)
www.christiansinaction.org

Cooperative Baptist Fellowship, Global Missions
www.thefellowship.info/globalmissions

CrossWorld (formerly UFM)
www.crossworld.org

Cumberland Presbyterian Church, Board of Missions
www.cumberland.org/bom

Deaf Missions
www.deafmissions.com

Epic Partners (see OneStory)

Evangel Bible Translators (EBT)
evangelbible.org

Evangelical Congregational Church,
Division of Missions
www.eccenter.com

Evangelical Presbyterian Church,
World Outreach Committee
www.epc.org

Faith Academy
www.faith.edu.ph

The General Board of Global Ministries,
United Methodist Church
www.gbgm-umc.org

Ghana Institute of Linguistics,
Literacy and Bible Translation (GILLBT)
www.gillbt.org

The Gideons International
www.gideons.org

Global interAction (Australian Baptist)
www.globalinteraction.org.au

Gospel Missionary Union (see Avant Minisrries)

Graduate Institute of Applied Linguistics (GIAL)
www.gial.edu

Hosanna / Faith Comes By Hearing (FCBH)
www.hosanna.org
www.fcbh.org

Integrity Music
www.integritymusic.com

International Bible Society
www.ibs.org

International Mission Board (IMB),
Southern Baptist
www.imb.org

JAARS
www.jaars.org

Japan Deaf Evangelical Mission (J-DEM)
www.j-dem.net

JESUS Film Project
www.jfp@ccci.org

The John M. Perkins Foundation (JMPF)
www.jmpf.org

Lutheran Bible Translators Canada (LBT)
www.lbtc.ca

Mercy Ships, OM
www.mercyships.org

Messengers of Christ
(See Lutheran Bible Translators)

Mission Aviation Fellowship (MAF USA)
www.maf.org

Mission Aviation Fellowship (MAF Australia)
www.maforg.au

The Mission Society for United Methodists
www.msum.org

Missionary Church, Inc.
www.mcusa.org

Nazarene Mission International
www.nazarenemissions.org

Netherlands Reformed Congregations (NRC)
(Nederlands Gereformeerde Kerken)
www.ngk.nl/ngken.html

New Tribes Mission (NTM)
www.ntm.org

OMF Canada
www.ca.omf.org

OneStory partners
www.ccc.onestory.org

Open Doors Australia
www.opendoors.org.au

Operation Mobilization (OM)
www.usa.om.org

Pioneers of Australia
www.pioneers.org.au

Presbyterian Church in America,
Mission to the World
www.mtw.org

Reformed Church in America
www.rca.org

Reformed Presbyterian Church of North America
www.rpforeignmissions.org

Regions Beyond Missionary Union (RBMU)
(see World Team)

Samaritan's Purse
www.samaritanspurse.org

Scripture Sign Project
www.gospelvideos.com

The Seed Company (TSC)
www.theseedcompany.org

SIL International
www.sil.org

SIM (Serving in Mission)
www.sim.org

Southern Methodist Church
www.southernmethodistchurch.org

Translation Association of the Philippines (TAP)
www.adnamis.org

TransWorld Radio (TWR)
www.twr.org

Unevangelized Fields Mission (see CrossWorld)

Uniting Church (Australia)
www.uca.org.au

ViBi (see Japan Evangelical Deaf Mission)

WEC International
www.wec-int.org

World Team
www.worldteam.org

Wycliffe Associates UK
www.wycliffeassociates.org.uk

Wycliffe Australia
www.wycliffe.org.au

Wycliffe Bible Translators (WBT)
www.wycliffe.org

Wycliffe Russia
www.wycliffe.ru

Appendix B
Together We Did! and
Together We Do!

Bible College of Victoria, Australia,
Mission Aviation Course

The Mission Aviation Course of the Bible College of Victoria (BCV), in Lilydale near Melbourne, began in 1995. The only mission aviation training in the southern hemisphere, it is operated in partnership with MAF Australia and JAARS. Students attend Bible and Mission lectures on the BCV campus but all aviation training takes place at BCV's Mission Aviation Center at Coldstream, located ten minutes from their Lilydale campus. Using aviation technologies, the course prepares men and women to serve in mission. Bible, mission, and practical ministry are integrated into the course along with the aviation training. Graduates are equipped to minister effectively as pilots or aircraft engineers within a mission aviation context. During its eleven-year history, students have enrolled in the Missions Aviation Course from twenty-one different countries.

Bible League

Bible League, founded in the late 1930s as the American Home Bible League, later became The World Home Bible League, reflecting their history of placing Scripture in Bibleless homes. Bible League's mission statement reads: "We are called by God to provide Scriptures and training worldwide, so that people prepared by the Holy Spirit will be brought into fellowship with Christ and His church." Today they work with local churches in more than 50 countries. They then make sure those Scriptures are used by the local church for evangelism, discipleship and church growth. If no local church exists, they train Christians to establish new churches.

Part of providing Scriptures is soliciting funds to publish Scriptures translated by Bible translators worldwide. Along with Wycliffe USA, Bible League participates in over 90% of all translations done by Wycliffe personnel.

Hosanna / Faith Comes by Hearing (FCBH)

To fulfill the Great Commission, the main ministry thrust of Evangel Bible Translators, Lutheran Bible Translators, Pioneer Bible Translators, and Wycliffe Bible Translators is putting God's Word into the mother tongue of people groups into written form. Their belief is that people need the Word in their mother tongue to come to faith and grow into mature Christians. Hosanna is committed to putting those translations of the Word done by these or other organizations into audio form so that those unable to read can, as they say, "hear God's Word in the language they pray in—their heart language." Hosanna works with missions and organizations in over seventy countries. In the USA, almost 50,000 churches from more than 100 denominations have participated in the FCBH program.

The JESUS Film Project and The Luke Partnership

The JESUS Film Project is a ministry of Campus Crusade for Christ (CCC). Wycliffe Bible Translators and CCC work together to produce the *JESUS* film, first produced by Inspirational Films in 1979. Wycliffe staff translate the Gospel of Luke first in their program, and The JESUS Film Project produces the *JESUS* film, a paraphrase of Luke's Gospel.

The Luke Partnership is a joint effort by The JESUS Film Project and The Seed Company (TSC). Katy Barnwell, former Wycliffe International Translation Coordinator, now with TSC, coordinates macro team workshops to train national translators. After these men and women, representing some of the larger Bibleless people groups, are trained in Bible translation, they translate the Gospel of Luke into their language. The JESUS Film Project then produces *JESUS* films using their translations.

Representatives from The JESUS Film Project, YWAM, the International Mission Board, Wycliffe and The Seed Company regularly meet together with other mission agencies to plan and pray about ways to ensure that unreached people groups all over the world have an opportunity to hear about Christ. Hundreds of people groups are still without some type of Christian witness.

Lutheran Bible Translators (LBT)

In the '60s, before Lutheran Bible Translators was a sending organization, those who wanted to serve overseas with LBT worked under Wycliffe as associate members with their support coming through LBT. Since LBT does not have an Aviation arm, today, as in the early days, LBT missionaries depend on SIL and MAF.

As they have from the beginning, LBT translators from the North American continent continue to receive linguistic training at summer SIL schools and now also at the SIL Graduate Institute of Applied Linguistics (GIAL) in Dallas, TX, or at the Canada Institute of Linguistics (CanIL) in Langley, British Colombia.

Mission Aviation Fellowship (MAF)

MAF was founded in the USA in 1945. Later MAF UK and MAF Australia, separate organizations from MAF USA, came into being. Over the years, numerous mission organizations around the world have depended on MAF pilots to transport them and their cargo.

MAF Australia describes itself as "a not-for-profit team of

aviation professionals, who provide air transport in places of deepest human need—remote places where flying is not a luxury, but a lifeline. For over 50 years, MAF has flown over jungles, mountains, swamps and deserts to bring people medical care, emergency relief, long-term development and Christian hope."

OneStory partners

Campus Crusade for Christ International, International Mission Board (IMB), Youth With A Mission (YWAM), TransWorld Radio (TWR) and Wycliffe have come together under the name OneStory (formerly Epic Partners International) and created a two-year internship program called Quest. Designed for age 20 and older young people, Quest offers mission experience with an oral preference people group. With no written language, such groups are, by necessity, oral communicators and oral learners. A team of two works alongside mother-tongue story tellers to produce a panorama of Scripture in story form in the language of the people. This set of chronological Bible stories serves as an evangelistic tool and may become a stepping stone to the start of a translation program in the language.

Voices of the Faithful, a one-year devotional book, with Beth Moore; Kim P. Davis, compiling editor; Integrity Publishers, 2005, tells of an Aukaner man in a remote village whose first exposure to God's Word was listening to stories on tape. The January 7th devotion reads: "When people ... best benefit from hearing stories instead of reading them, IMB missionaries use a method called chronological Bible storying." The tapes, narrated by an Aukaner speaker, tell the foundational Bible stories from Creation to the Ascension. God gave the Aukaner man a dream in which Jesus called out to him, "Come." He had listened to the tapes many times. Then he listened to that voice and came into a relationship with Jesus!

Russian Missions Festival

In the fall of 2005, Operation Mobilization (OM) and Wycliffe Russia (WR) partnered to offer a "Missions Festival" in St. Petersburg, Russia—the first ever held in that country. Besides OM and WR, 15 other organizations (including two radio stations, three Christian colleges, six publishing houses and a gift company operated by Christians) cooperated to organize the festival. Most of the 600 who attended were young people, plus pastors and other church members. About a hundred of the attendees represented 27 different missions and other Christian organizations. The hope is that this will form the foundation of a unified effort to reach, train, and mobilize Russian people to become active participants in Bible translation and in the work of other ministries, first in St. Petersburg, then in western Russia.

Samaritan's Purse

Some may consider Operation Christmas Child as "what Samaritan's Purse does." And it is. But it is only one of many things the organization does. Through this program, "shoeboxes" (filled with toys, candy, toothpaste, soap—and Scripture portions) are solicited and then delivered by Samaritans Purse (or to different organizations who deliver them) to children around the world each Christmas. The organizations and churches worldwide which cooperate in this mammoth undertaking are too numerous to mention.

One mission in Papua New Guinea delivered Operation Christmas Child boxes to villages along a highway where there was always danger of cars being stopped and people robbed—sometimes at gunpoint. Since that time, far fewer incidents have occurred.

But as wonderful a program as Operation Christmas Child is, Samaritan's Purse does much more than this one program.

On their web site it says: "Our work takes us throughout the world to extend the love of Jesus Christ to hurting people. For over 35 years, Samaritan's Purse has done our utmost to follow Christ's command by giving to the aid of the world's poor, sick, and suffering . . . in countries around the world with food, medicine and other assistance in the Name of Jesus Christ. This, in turn, earns us a hearing for the Gospel, the Good News of eternal life through Jesus Christ."

Wycliffe and Samaritan's Purse have a long-standing working-together relationship—from involvement in Operation Christmas

Child to flying and servicing Samaritan's Purse airplanes and helicopters in hurricane and tsunami relief.

In 1999, after a major hurricane swept through Honduras, Don Archibald, then manager of SIL Aviation in Papua New Guinea, helped Samaritan's Purse purchase a Bell Long Ranger 3 helicopter. Roy Harris (formerly with SIL, now with Samaritan's Purse) flew that helicopter for Samaritan's Purse in their humanitarian aid to the victims of the Honduras hurricane. And JAARS aircraft technicians provided the maintenance and ground support for that project. Recently, several JAARS aircraft maintenance technicians serviced Samaritan's Purse helicopters in tsunami stricken areas, and a JAARS pilot flew one of those helicopters for Samaritan's Purse.

In the past, JAARS Aviation personnel installed radios and a cargo compartment and did a number of other modifications on a twin-engine King Air that was used by Samaritan's Purse for service in Alaska.

Appendix C
Ministries of the JMPF
for Reconciliation and
Development

Mendenhall Ministries

When Dr. Perkins returned from California to New Hebron, Mississippi, where he had grown up, he founded a program in Mendenhall to empower his people in the rural areas, enabling them to meet their own needs and thus move beyond poverty. As president of this ministry, he established a church, a health center, a school, a thrift store and developed a housing program. Today Mendenhall Ministries thrives under the leadership of Artis Fletcher and Darel Thigpen.

The Voice of Calvary Ministries

Twelve years later, Dr. Perkins moved to Jackson, Mississippi. There he developed The Voice of Calvary Ministries, which focused on evangelism, social action and community development for inner-city families. Like the Mendenhall Ministries, the Voice of Calvary Ministries also consisted of a church, health center, thrift store and included housing development. One of the main ministries of Voice of Calvary Ministries: to teach and inspire people to carry the Gospel around the country. After ten years, Voice of Calvary was turned over to Lem Tucker.

The Harambee Christian Family Center and the Harambee Preparatory School

God led the Perkins to move back to Pasadena, California. The community they lived in there had one of the highest daytime crime rates in the city. "Crime and violence were common happenings. Crack and cocaine were just hitting the market and young people were killing each other at an alarming rate," Dr. Perkins says. Houses were purchased in the neighborhood and the Harambee Christian Family Center was established to serve not only African-American families but also Latino families. In 1995, on the same property with that center, Pricilla Perkins and Julie Ragland, introduced Harambee Preparatory School. HPS provides children from poverty level homes a quality academic education. Today the school is under the leadership of Rudy Carrasco and his wife.

Christian Community Development Association

In 1989, Dr. Perkins called together a group of Christian leaders bonded by one significant commitment: expressing the love of Christ in America's poor communities at the grass-roots level. The Christian Community Development Association (CCDA), established at that time with 37 founding members, now has a national and an international membership. In the U.S., CCDA has expanded its ministry into more than 100 cities and townships, bringing people together to duplicate what Dr. Perkins first started.

Each year a CCDA Institute draws around 3,000 people where they are taught and trained to carry the Gospel around the world. One such CCDA Institute at Seattle Pacific University, called the John Perkins Center for Reconciliation, Leadership Training, and Community Development, is directed by W. Tali Hairston.

The Spencer Perkins Center for Reconciliation and Youth Development

This center honors the key player God used to bring Dr. Perkins to Himself: his son Spencer. After Spencer's death in

1998, the Perkins family moved back to Jackson, Mississippi. That year construction began on The Spencer Perkins Center for Reconciliation and Youth Development. "Our mission" says Dr. Perkins, "is to train and equip a new generation of indigenous leaders who are driven by the love of God to pass on the torch of reconciliation and youth development here and around the world." The program is continuing to develop under of the leadership of their daughter, Elizabeth Perkins. Two of their sons work with her in this ministry. "My goal is to see this place become a center of training for young people and adults. We plan to see a senior daycare center and a K–6 prep school established," says Dr. Perkins.

The Zechariah 8 project

Recently with his daughter Elizabeth, Dr. Perkins initiated the Zechariah 8 project in West Jackson, Mississippi. Their goal for this project is to stabilize the community, to reduce the movement of single parent families. They are buying and remodeling older homes with the goal of making them available for families to own.

Appendix D
Wycliffe USA Cooperative Agreement Summaries

The following groups have signed "Cooperative Agreements" with Wycliffe USA. In most cases, individuals under these agreements are members of both their denominational mission agency and Wycliffe USA.

As dual members:

- They participate in the Wycliffe USA training program.
- Most are under Wycliffe USA payroll and benefit plans with some agreements providing the agency's group benefit plan as an option.
- Some agreements have members under Wycliffe USA jurisdiction on the field and under the respective agency's jurisdiction (or dual jurisdiction) when on furlough.

- Raising financial support for ministry is done in denominational churches in coordination with the mission agency. Support of the denominational agency in this area varies with some agencies actively endorsing the individuals within its churches, to some taking full responsibility for the individual's financial support.

1. Assemblies of God World Missions

2. Associate Reformed Presbyterian Church, World Witness—Board of Foreign Missions

3. Bible Fellowship Church Board of Missions

4. Baptist General Conference Board of World Missions

5. Cooperative Baptist Fellowship, Global Missions

6. Evangelical Congregational Church Division of Missions

7. Presbyterian Church in America, Mission To the World

8. Missionary Church, Inc.

9. The Mission Society for United Methodists

10. Cumberland Presbyterian Church, Board of Missions

11. Evangelical Presbyterian Church,
    World Outreach Committee

12. Reformed Presbyterian Church of N. America—
    Board of Foreign Missions

13. Reformed Church in America

14. Southern Methodist Church

Information received from:
Cooperative Agreement Coordinator
Wycliffe USA, Orlando
1-800-992-5433 ext. 4129
doug_haag@Wycliffe.org

About the Author

Real People Eat Sweet Potato

"Tu-tu-tu! Tu-tu-tu!" up from the 2000-foot incline, the bamboo flute sounded. Umahto had just announced to the village that his river traps had yielded an eel.

Oh, for a bit of eel to supplement our day-after-day sweet potato and greens diet, I thought. "Maybe Umahto will share some with us," I told Ed as I prepared to walk over to Umahto's part of the village.

I found Umahto sitting under a shade tree, surrounded by an audience. Banana leaves were spread on the ground and his eel was displayed for all to admire. . .

"*Naniboe, anotah kawerone* (My father, you did very well)," I said. No comment. "My husband and I really like eel!" *That ought to do it. The Awas are always pleased that we like their food.* That did "do it."

"My daughter," he said, "I would give you some eel if I wasn't obligated to give it all to my new daughter-in-law's parents. But here's some sweet potato . . ."

That evening, as we roasted sweet potato in our open fire, a few Awas sat with us on our woven-bamboo floor. Umahto wandered in, just as our once-a-week treat was done. When we first began cooking Ed's unique brand of *fudge*—sugar, cocoa and water—it tasted "Yuck!" to the Awa people. But no longer.

Umahto urged me to "Put some *sokoreti* (chocolate) right here in the palm of my hand," then replied to my concern, "No, it won't burn me . . . my hands are tough."

"My father," I said, "I would give you some *sokoreti* if I wasn't obligated to give it to my poor, hungry husband. But . . . I can give you sweet potato, and it's even roasted."

Umahto laughed so hard that I was afraid he'd fall into the fire.

A few short years before, Ed and I had come to live among the Awa people. We didn't look like them, and we certainly could not dress like them. We could and did enjoy their "daily bread"—sweet potato. And we were striving hard to learn to speak like them and to understand how they thought. Our goal was not just to translate Scripture into their language, but also to become friends with them and to introduce our friend Jesus to them.

The Awas had a hard time accepting that we were real people, rather than spirits. "God wants you to love *real* people, not *ideal* people," says Rick Warren in *The Purpose Driven Life*. Evenings spent around the fire eating their sweet potato, helped establish that we were real people.

That was a vital step to telling them about our friend Jesus, the "Sweet Potato of Life," the One who was both a real person and the one and only real God.

The Lovings served with Wycliffe in the Highlands of Papua New Guinea among a group of people who had never heard the name of Jesus. Living in an Awa village, they learned the beautiful tonal language of the Awas. With their help, they translated the New Testament and a book of Old Testament Bible stories. The people's acceptance of the Gospel has resulted in churches in most Awa villages.

Aretta has been writing since she was seven years old. Her appreciative audience of one—her mother—always encouraged her. She lived long enough to see her daughter publish articles in numerous Christian magazines, including "Decision." At Biola, Aretta was mission column editor of the college paper. After graduating from Biola with a BA in education, she took the one-year School of Missionary Medicine course, now Biola Nursing School.

Aretta's book *Slices of Life*, YWAM Publishing, 2000, contains short, inspirational stories from Papua New Guinea, and from Kenya, where the Lovings also served for over four years. *Slices* has been published in Russian by Wycliffe Russia and Chinese by Wycliffe Hong Kong. Aretta also authored *Zoeter dan Honing* (*Sweeter than Honey*), published by Wycliffe Netherlands, 2004.

Today the Lovings live in North Carolina near the JAARS Center, which supports Wycliffe work in over 60 countries around the world, and often helps other mission organizations.

You may contact Aretta at: Aretta_Loving@sil.org to schedule her for speaking engagements.

About the Author's Call to Mission Work

"The summer before I turned twelve, at American Missionary Fellowship Bible camp, I slept outdoors under California redwoods at night, heard God's Word proclaimed each morning and swam in the Russian River each afternoon. There I came to know Jesus as Savior. The next summer at camp, I told God I wanted to be a missionary. My commitment never wavered," Aretta says.

"When I was in high school, Mom told me to take typing. 'I'm going to be a missionary, not a secretary,' " I said. Aretta is glad Mom won. "I typed the New Testament about five times!"

Available from
Harvest Day Books

Bible Translation/Mission Work/Commitment

$15.95

Jungle Jewels & Jaguars
Living with the Amueshas Translating God's Word
By Martha Tripp

The true story of a young woman's journey deep into the jungles of Peru to live with the native Amuesha tribe, learn their language, and bring to them the Word of God in their native tongue. This amazing memoir brings us the trials and triumphs of this 23-year Bible translation mission.

Power of Prayer with Scripture/Life-Change

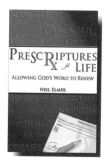

$15.95

PreScriptures for Life
Allowing God's Word to Renew
By Neil Elmer

Prescriptures for Life is about tapping into God's power to overcome obstacles that get in the way of moving forward in life. This user-friendly book provides pertinent Scripture in a topical format. Easy-to-use and share with a friend.

Order at www.ReadingUp.com

Power of God's Word/Inspiring Stories

$12.95

Together We Can!
A Mosaic of Stories and Devotions
Displaying the Impact of God's Word
By Aretta Loving

"*Together We Can!* brings us stories about the truth of God's Word, changed lives, miracles, and increased faith. The one thing they all have in common is the power of the Word of God..."
- Dr. John R. Watters,
Exec. Dir. Wycliffe International

Christ's Saving Grace from Rock Music Culture

$14.95

Rockin' Down the Highway to Hell
Discovering the Hidden Satanic
Power Behind Today's Music
By Michael Plont, Associate Pastor, Mt. Zion Church, Traverse City, Michigan

Exposes the perils, snares and hidden satanic power of the rock music culture—an eye-opener for high schoolers, parents, teachers, and anyone concerned about our youth and young adults. The author shares his testimony and points to Jesus Christ, Savior and Deliverer.

Order at www.ReadingUp.com

Incredible Testimony for Christ

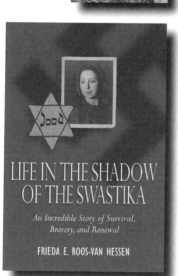

Life in the Shadow of the Swastika
An Incredible Story of Survival, Bravery, and Renewal
By Frieda E. Roos-van Hessen

Jewish Holocaust Survivor finds her Messiah after World War II while reading the Psalms of David and writings from the prophet Isaiah.

Frieda E. van Hessen was one of the world's top concert and opera singers. At 19, she sang the lead for the Dutch version of Walt Disney's *Snow White*. At 24, she was the soloist in a performance of Verdi's *Requiem* for the Dutch Royal Family. Frieda won the Grande Diplome at the World Contest in Geneva, Switzerland where judges said she was one of the eight best female singers in the world. The future could not have seemed brighter for Frieda until she was forced into hiding when the Nazis invaded Holland during World War II.

This book tells of her hiding, miraculous escapes, and her determination to survive some of the worst horrors this world has ever seen.

$15.95

Order at www.ReadingUp.com

Order Form

For additional copies of *Together We Can!*, or for any Harvest Day book, please fill out the following information or visit our website at www.ReadingUp.com. Discounts are available for bulk orders and to bookstores, libraries, and other retailers.

Fax orders:	(231)929-1993
Telephone orders:	(231)929-1999
E-mail orders:	Orders@BookMarketingSolutions.com
Postal orders:	BMS
	10300 E. Leelanau Court
	Traverse City, MI 49684

Please send the following Books: I understand that I may return any of them for a full refund—for any reason, no questions asked.

_____

_____

_____

Name: _____

Address: _____

City: _____ State: _____ Zip: _____ – _____

E-mail address: _____

Phone (in case we need to contact you) _____

Sales Tax: Please add 6% for products being shipped to Michigan addresses.
Shipping by air:
US: $4.50 for the first book and $0.50 for each additional book.
International: $9.00 for the first book and $5.00 for each additional book (estimate).

Payment: ☐ Check ☐ Credit Card:
☐ Visa ☐ AMEX ☐ MasterCard ☐ Discover

Card Number: _____

Name on Card: _____ Exp. Date: ____ / _____